Wolf Tourist

Wolf Tourist

One Summer in the West

Jay Robert Elhard

UTAH STATE UNIVERSITY PRESS
Logan, Utah

for my parents

Utah State University Press
Logan, Utah 84322-7800

Library of Congress Cataloging-in-Publication Data

Elhard, Jay Robert, 1961-
  Wolf tourist : one summer in the West / Jay Robert Elhard.
    p. cm.
  Includes bibliographical references
  ISBN 0-87421-211-1
  1. Wolves—Yellowstone National Park. 2. Wildlife reintroduction—
Yellowstone National Park. 3. Wolves—Yellowstone National Park—Public
opinion. 4. Wildlife reintroduction—Yellowstone National Park—Public
opinion. I. Title.
QL737.C22E58 1996
599.74'442—dc20   96-10024
                                                     CIP

Contents

Prologue

I've never seen a wolf—zoo beasts are not to be counted; they are ultimately no more interesting than dead carp, sullen, furtive, morose. Perhaps I'll never see a wolf. And I don't offer this little problem as central to anyone but myself.

—Jim Harrison, *Wolf: A False Memoir*, 1971

Home

MY FAVORITE SOUVENIR OF THE SUMMER OF 1993 WAS A WHITE ceramic mug loaded with more irony than its maker probably intended. There was a wide, wilderness landscape painted across the sides, and a familiar name, YELLOW-STONE NATIONAL PARK, was stenciled near the top. At rest, at room temperature, the foreground was filled with silhouettes of black, flat spruce trees. At work, while the mug held hot brews of coffee, tea or cider, this timberline turned translucent, slowly revealing sketches of two gray wolves, one sitting to the left on its haunches, howling with its nose pointed into a yellow sky, the other trotting to the right with its face turned squarely to the world. Descriptive phrases appeared eventually above their heads, too—*Calling Home, Coming Home*. Then, inevitably, each time the mug's contents cooled or were emptied, these two wolves and their supposed thoughts of a place long remembered came to be cloaked again by darkening layers of trees. I've always assumed that the designer of this mug meant to mimic the elusiveness of wolves in the wild or, perhaps, to portray a recent change in the outlook for their official return to Yellowstone. Yet, for me, it also has served as a fitting reflection of human attitudes toward wolves over the last 400 years—hot and cold mostly, rarely tepid.

I am writing now from Ohio in the winter of 1996, as it happens, right around the time that federal officials out West are transplanting a second batch of gray wolves from Canada into the wilds of Yellowstone National Park and central Idaho. Last winter, after more than two decades of prior debate and controversy, a first wave of twenty-nine animals was set loose in the two areas. By the following spring, as some locals had hoped and others dreaded, pups were born—in Yellowstone's case, the first known inside the park in upwards of seventy years.

Recently, biologists running the program have started hinting in the press that this year's group of thirty-five or so transplants might be the last they may need to bring down from Canada to make an eventual success of wolf recovery in the region. Originally, groups of animals were to have been shipped south for three, four, maybe even five consecutive winters. Last year, though, more pups turned up than expected—in Yellowstone, the number was as high as nine—and more adults survived than expected. While, at the outset, the first-year mortality rate was forecast to run as high as 30 percent, the actual number ranged between 17 and 24 percent—somewhere between five and seven deaths out of those first twenty-nine animals.

At least two, it turns out, were shot and killed by the local citizenry—one in Idaho less than ten days and sixty miles from where it had been first dropped off; the other outside Yellowstone's northeast entrance by a man who evidently had made plans to have the head stuffed and mounted afterwards. Two more are missing in Idaho, maybe due to malfunctions in the electronic collars biologists use to track them, but more likely, as at least one newspaper I read suggested, because they died in some fashion. Two others expired in apparent roadway mishaps—one was run over by a Park Service delivery truck; the other was found dead of unknown causes recently beside a state highway near Daniel, Wyoming—something like 130 miles south of the park, where it had been spotted last, almost eight weeks earlier. The final and most significant fatality of the seven possible was an animal that was shot by federal agents earlier this month as a consequence of a longstanding promise to local ranchers about what would become of transplants that made a habit of tangling with animals grazing on private land outside Yellowstone. It was, and so far remains, the only confirmed instance of livestock depredation since the recovery program began in earnest a little more than a year ago.

Last month, in early January 1996, the story goes, a young male—maybe a bit swayed by the effects of the oncoming breeding season to find a mate and territory of its own—broke from its pack inside Yellowstone and ventured north into the Paradise Valley to a sheep operation just south of Emigrant, Montana. Within two days of reports that two sheep had been killed, federal agents tracked the "rogue" by radio signals from its collar, fired a net over it from a helicopter and hauled it away, tranquilized, to an enclosure back in Yellowstone's Lamar Valley. The owners of the dead sheep, meanwhile, received assurance of cash compensation for their losses from a $100,000 fund mustered for such purposes by the conservationist group, Defenders of Wildlife. Three weeks later, the same wolf returned to the same herd and at least two more sheep were reported missing. Federal officials then invoked the full authority of an amendment Congress made to the Endangered Species Act in 1982—a provision which allows much more flexible control of designated *experimental populations* of an otherwise fully-protected species—and summarily dispatched and discharged this critter as a potential contributor to the recovery plan's gene pool. So now, I suppose, for those who care to keep score, the body count around the two recovery areas combined stands at something like—*wolves 7, sheep 4, humans 0.*

There's a dead dog to figure into the balance somewhere, too. In late December, one of Yellowstone's three established packs took a foray well beyond park boundaries and—as wolves are often known to do in such encounters—took out a hunting dog along the way. By and large, though, biologists have said that the park's new wolves are dieting almost exclusively on elk—as well as an occasional moose or mountain goat. They also report that despite their reputation as an especially reclusive species, wolves once made public appearances in the Lamar Valley on forty-three consecutive days last summer, fueling an 18 percent increase in tourist traffic through Yellowstone's northeast entrance and nearby Cooke City, Montana. For the first time in the park's history, apparently, grizzly bears were displaced last year as the one animal visitors asked to see most in Yellowstone. Wolves, just as economic studies projected, have come to be far and away the park's top animal attraction.

Public enthusiasm for the wolf's return to the region could hardly be characterized as unanimous, though. Ever since Interior Secretary Bruce Babbitt first signed the recovery plan into action in the spring of 1994, there have been occasional flurries of legal and legislative counter-maneuvering reported in the three states surrounding the park. In Wyoming, lawmakers once advocated fixing a $500 bounty on wolves and ordering the state attorney to defend anyone that federal prosecutors might accuse of killing a wolf. In Montana, legislators considered a resolution to reintroduce wild, free-ranging wolves to the confines of Central Park in Manhattan and San Francisco's Presidio. In Idaho, one elected representative suggested, apparently not entirely in jest, that his state should secede from the union to solve its wolf difficulties. The first reintroduction process was delayed twice with lawsuits filed by the Wyoming Farm Bureau—once as the animals were arriving as caged freight at their respective release sites. Critical field preparations in Canada for this year's transplant were threatened when a senator from Montana was able to cut $200,000 out of the program's funding during a protracted budget standoff between the White House and Congress. Groundwork was permitted to continue only after three environmental groups—led, again, by Defenders of Wildlife—stepped forward with money to sustain the operation. Then, as recently as a few weeks ago, on the very day that news broke about the discovery of dead sheep in Paradise Valley, Montana Governor Marc Raicot called upon federal agencies to abandon all further reintroduction efforts because they no longer made sense and any success that could be claimed with wolf recovery so far was being jeopardized.

There are, as always in America, other lawsuits pending as well. Last week, hearings were scheduled in federal court in Casper, Wyoming in a case that has joined three separate suits against the government filed by an unlikely collection of plaintiffs. The Sierra Club and National Audubon Society are challenging the *experimental* designation, asserting that wolves should be reintroduced to Yellowstone under the full protection of the Endangered Species Act. A second suit, filed by two residents of northwestern Wyoming, maintains that the transplants are of a different sub-species than native wolves they believe have survived in the region all along and that, as a consequence, the gene pool for these rare, some say mythical, indigenous animals is being threatened by the exotic creatures the government is importing from Canada. A third suit, filed by the American Farm Bureau and other commodity groups, contends that the whole program is bogus to the core because more than 52,000 wolves already exist just fine up in Canada and northern Montana and that, in effect, the initial listing of the gray wolf as endangered more than twenty years ago—which has required the government to protect it and promote its recovery ever since—is an old, politically-motivated error of bureaucracy that simply has never been rectified.

The wolf's status as endangered in the region indeed is supposed to be lifted eventually. As things were first outlined in a formal proposal three years ago, federal control over the plan would be turned over to existing state and tribal agencies once a hundred or so wolves persist in each recovery area, or rather, to cite the government's official standard, once ten wolf packs have produced litters of pups in each area for three straight years. At the time, officials believed that day could come as early as the year 2002, after a total estimated expense of $6.7 million. Still—whether or not this year's transplants from Canada wind up being the last, and whether the wolf's endangered status is ultimately determined by the courts next month or by events in the wild in the next millennium—I suspect that the presence of actual wolves in the region will probably always refuse to become old news, at least so long as westerners themselves continue to choose sides between Old and New West, between tradition and science, between informed friends and unenlightened enemies, based, sometimes solely, on whether somebody is likely to share or oppose their ideas about wolves.

Not long ago, in my reading, I discovered that Edward Hoagland encountered much the same notion in his essay "Lament The Red Wolf" about another flavor of wolf in another part of the United States back in 1974—

> The most vivid observation to be made about animal enthusiasts—both the professionals who work in the field and, in particular, the amateurs—is that they are split between the rosiest, well-adjusted sort of souls and the wounded and lame. (More professionals are rosy, more amateurs are lame.) Animals used to provide a lowlife way to kill and get away with it, as they do still, but, more intriguingly, for some people they are an aperture through which wounds drain. The scapegoat of olden times, driven off for the bystanders' sins, has become a tender thing, a running injury. There, running away—save it, save it—is me; hurt it and you are hurting me.
>
> Wolves are well suited to cupping any wounds that we wish to be drained. Big and concise enough to command the notice of any dullard, they are aggressive, as the wounded themselves wish to be aggressive. Once passionately persecuted, in just the turnabout which people relish, a wolf can now be taken to represent the very Eden we miss, and being a wolf, is thought to be the best at what it does in a world which demands that any creature to receive attention must be the "best."

Clearly, by Hoagland's measure, I, too, would rank among
the amateurs, a lame soul drawn into stories about a
charismatic animal for all the wrong reasons. Plenty of
books, articles and opinions, after all, have been rendered
on wolves and the Yellowstone controversy in recent years.
(Readers are urged unequivocally to consider a range of
authorities listed here as "selected readings.") If there is
one slim claim this work can make to legitimacy, though,
it's a federal provision requiring that local cultural values
be appraised as a part of any proposal for lasting environmental action. In this case, that proposal was a Draft
Environmental Impact Statement (DEIS) the government
published in July 1993 as a first, formal step toward reintroducing wolves to Yellowstone. In the end, almost three
years later, I've decided that what followed was probably
less about wolves than it was about people restlessly chasing their ideas of wolves. Truth, in this instance, turned
out to be one gray, slippery critter.

—February 1996

Wolf Country

If the wolf is to survive, the wolf haters must be outnumbered. They must be outshouted, outfinanced, and outvoted. Their narrow and biased attitude must be outweighed by an attitude based on an understanding of natural processes. Finally their hate must be outdone by a love for the whole of nature, for the unspoiled wilderness, and for the wolf as a beautiful, interesting and integral part of both.

—L. David Mech, *The Wolf: The Ecology and Behavior Of An Endangered Species*, 1969

Men, it has been well said, think in herds; it will be seen that they go mad in herds, while they only recover their senses slowly, and one by one.

—Charles Mackay, *Extraordinary Popular Delusions and the Madness of Crowds*, 1852

Park Falls, Wisconsin

MONDAY MORNING IN JUNE, LATE, AFTER RIDING DOWN MILES OF knotty backroads through patches of Wisconsin's once great northern forest, Adrian P. Wydeven, the state's highest-ranking wildlife biologist for nongame species, slowed his Ford Bronco to a walking pace and allowed a plume of dust that had risen in the truck's wake to overtake him. He steered with his head hanging out the window, the truck drifting sideways, then true again, while he concentrated fully on bits of earth moving directly below. Tangled in the passenger seat beside him, I looked out and down, too, but to my eyes everything that passed beneath the wheels just then still looked like dirt. Pale, plain and lots of it.

"Trap right there," Wydeven said, maybe more to the side of his truck than to me. Then again moments later, he said, "Trap right there. There's a *scat* right there."

"Scat" is a fast, polite, scientific way of saying wild animal droppings. A monarch butterfly balanced on the pile Wydeven had just noticed. Butterflies are drawn to nutrients and moisture lingering in fresh scat. I told Wydeven, or at least what I could see of the back of his dangling head, what I had heard recently about the government biologists around here, that they had somehow trained butterflies at great expense to light on wolf scat to expedite their tracking surveys. Those flashy wings, I said, are supposed to serve as field markers. Wydeven let the truck coast with his foot poised above the brake, silent, as if I had said nothing at all, then inched the truck's gears back into a gallop before picking up the conversation again right where he had left off.

"That's a good sign. It means a wolf has gone through here recently."

For a time, I hoped Wydeven hadn't heard me just then, that my stab at wildlife potty humor would pass unnoticed, but he soon mentioned that his partner on this particular trapping project, Ron Schultz, had done his master's research on wolf scat. Schultz had spent years collecting hundreds of scat samples, measuring, cataloging and analyzing them all based on diameter, condition and content. Wolf scat, Wydeven said, is vital to the work of government trackers, trappers and wildlife managers. It says a lot about what a wolf's been eating lately and when it made its last kill.

Wolves may eat well only once every few days or weeks, and, as a result, they have developed digestive tracts that are accustomed to long stretches of famine and feast. In the first twelve hours after gorging on a new kill, for instance, their scat is black and watery. Wolves typically bolt down as much as fifteen or twenty pounds of meat in the first sitting alone, in some cases, almost a fifth of their own body weight. In the early going, they're swallowing chunks of choice rations, whole organs and high-energy fat their bodies are especially good at metabolizing, so in the end, there isn't much left of anything firm for butterflies to find. By the second or third day of going back and chewing on the lesser-grade leftovers, however, a wolf's scat becomes more formed and lighter in color, like that sample Wydeven had noticed a mile or two back. More of the dead animal's hair and bones begins to show up in wolf scat around about day four and five. After seven days or so, when there might be nothing left of a kill but an untidy pile of bones, a wolf's scat is white with a bit of green sprinkled through it from digested calcium. Wolf intestines have a way of wrapping hair from the hides they eat around the sharp edges of bones passing through their digestive tracts. Some of the wolf scat Wydeven described to me sounded so hairy and layered I might have expected them to sprout toes and scamper into the underbrush. If enough time passes between fresh kills for wolves, scavengers and rival predators to finish off a carcass, Wydeven said, nothing is left behind, not even blood-red soaked snow.

Wydeven spoke between bites of his own lunch now, peanut butter on whole-grain bread and apple juice out of a box. He jammed the wrappings into a compartment under the dashboard filled with detailed topographic maps, a magnetic compass and a couple of kids' toys—a yellow rubber bear and a neon pink plastic leg-hold trap about the size of a fifty-cent piece. The latter didn't look as if it was meant to be a working replica. Its exaggerated, serrated jaws flopped lightly in my palm when I first picked it up. Once Wydeven noticed and said it belonged to one of his boys, though, I put it back. It had its place and, for a moment I had evidently forgotten, so did I.

I had stopped in Wisconsin, in part, to visit a place where wolves actually lived at present, to bone up on their history and habits, and also, in part, because I understood wolves were recovering here largely of their own volition. Most people believed that the wolves living around here these days had migrated south from Minnesota, recolonizing old range bit by bit as their northern ranks expanded. Others—including Wydeven's trapping partner Ron Schultz, I would come to find—suspected Wisconsin's wolves might be the descendants of a handful of remnant native animals that had somehow survived outside human notice in the state all along. Both views, it so happened, were being advanced farther west that summer to explain recent sightings of wolves around Yellowstone.

The state of Wisconsin asks specific conditions of guest researchers and media people who want to ride along on a wolf trapline. Observers are not allowed out of the truck at any time while traps are planted by roadsides and checked each day. This precaution is not so much for the observer's safety as it is because human beings have a tendency to leave behind a wash of distinct smells in the woods. A wolf's olfactory area is some fourteen times larger than that of humans and its sense of smell may well be up to a hundred times more sensitive. Wolves are known to adopt stretches of outlying roads as runways. Sometimes it's because they offer fast and safe commutes. Other times it's because roads and their drainages interrupt dark forest canopies much like meadows, fostering light and low-lying plants which, in turn, attract deer and other animals that wolves are willing to chase and eat. Wolves plying a living on such terrain have apparently grown used to odors left by occasional cars—whiffs of exhaust, imprints of tire rubber and a few spatterings of fuel, lubricants, coolants and brake fluid. What wolves may be less accustomed to smelling in such places, however, are indications of people actually tramping around outside their cars and, in particular, the battery of chemicals they tend to use as part of their personal hygiene regimens. Even though they won't be let outside the truck to mingle with the elements, guests to the trapline are told to shower each morning without soaps and shampoos and to apply no hint whatsoever of deodorant, hair tonic or cosmetics.

Wydeven himself, for that matter, seemed to make a point of climbing into the same set of clothes each day I rode along on his trapline—a gray shirt, heavy canvas pants with loops for tools built into the sides, a leather knife sheaf strapped above his right hip. I gathered that spreading fresh tones even of laundry soap, starch and fabric softener across a wolf's sensory landscape might give away Wydeven's passing presence around his traps that much sooner and make the job of catching it and fitting a radio collar around its neck that much harder.

Every effort associated with this trapline, after all, was directed toward the end of putting a radio collar on a healthy, wild wolf. Only after that happened could Wydeven and his colleagues track its movements more readily by air, van or backpack and, eventually, make better guesses about the extent of its territory, food preferences, breeding and denning status. As the man responsible for keeping tabs on all the wild critters that aren't subject to hunting in the state (including badgers, cougars, lynx, martens and flying squirrels, among others), Wydeven considered such details about individual wolves a precious commodity. It helped him determine if and when he should start trying to nudge lone wolves of breeding age closer together as potential mates, whether he should immunize them against outbreaks of disease and whether, even a quarter century after the last wolf bounties were scratched off the state's books, he had evidence of poachers still killing wolves inside his jurisdiction.

So far as anybody knows, neither the radio collars nor the catch-and-release trapping practice present much lasting harm to wolves. What they do represent, however, is a broader irony that wasn't lost on Wydeven. In order to promote the recovery of a free-ranging, pack-oriented endangered predator in his state, he needed to collar a good many of the individuals. More often than not, that meant he had to use a modified version of the same tool that helped eliminate them from so much of their former range. At a time when most government scientists were otherwise occupied with technologies tied to microscopes, satellites and computers, Wydeven was using tools based almost solely on the somewhat magical premise of fooling a wolf's formidable nose. Even after four centuries, North American ingenuity had yet to come up with a safer and more efficient means of catching a wolf than a spring-loaded steel boobytrap hidden in the ground.

Out here, where such contraptions are still being used, observers are expected to smell neutral or, in another sense, invisible. By extension then, they come to understand that they should behave invisibly, too, that they should not distract or get in the way of all the work that has to be done.

Among the things that surprised me most in the early going that summer was learning that despite their official designation as an endangered species, gray wolves, as a whole, have never truly faced an imminent threat of extinction. Wolves were once the most widely-dispersed land mammal on the planet, aside from humans, adapting to every ecological habitat in the northern hemisphere except tropical rain forests and arid deserts.

By 1993, there were at least 50,000 wolves running around Canada, maybe that many again in the former Soviet Union, more than 7,000 in Alaska, perhaps 2,000 combined in the states of Minnesota, Michigan, Wisconsin, Montana, Idaho and Washington and then more in the old countries of Europe and Asia, perhaps 2,000 in Spain and Portugal, 2,000 in Rumania, 900 in Poland, 400 in Italy, 200 in Hungary, 200 in Greece and even more still hanging onto pockets of habitat in Scandinavia, France, Germany, Czechoslovakia, Yugoslavia, Albania, Bulgaria, Turkey, Syria, Israel, Saudi Arabia, Iraq, Iran, Afghanistan and India.

Until recently, taxonomists recognized thirty-two distinct subspecies of the gray wolf (*Canis lupus*) around the world, twenty-four in North America alone. Since many of the old subspecies distinctions were based on geography, though, scientists funneled skull and skeletal measurements through computers and cut the total number of subspecies to ten—five in North America (*arctos, occidentalis, nubilus, baileyi* and *laycon*) and five in Eurasia (*albus, communis, lupus, cubanensis* and *pallipes*). The endangered red wolf (*Canis rufus*) of the southeastern United States is now considered a separate species unto itself, although it appears closely-related to *pallipes*, the gray wolf subspecies now found from Israel to India, the same race from which all domestic dogs probably descended about 12,000 years ago. The break happened just once, scientists now say, so technically even breeds of dogs that look more like yapping bats without wings are as closely-related genetically to wild wolves today as, say, more woodsy-looking malamutes and huskies. There is also a theory circulating of late which suggests all wolves descended originally from the red wolf in North America, that ancestors of today's wide-ranging gray wolf subspecies migrated to Asia and Europe, evolved into something closer to their contemporary forms and returned to establish themselves as top predators in food chains all the way south into what is now Mexico.

Aside from notable exceptions within those ten par-ticular subspecies—such as the now critically-endangered Mexican wolf, which exists at present only in captivity—the gray wolf's prompt classification as endangered in 1973, the first year the Endangered Species Act took full effect, came primarily because it had been scraped out of so much of its former range. Wolves have been subject to intense, ingenious and often pathological human persecu-tion in North America for more than 400 years. The first wolf bounty was enacted in the Massachusetts Colony in 1630—at a penny a wolf—and in ensuing centuries, wolves were shot, trapped, poisoned, clubbed and dyna-mited across the continent as a matter of course. Pups were buried alive in their dens. Captured animals were drawn and quartered with ropes and horses, doused with kerosene and set afire, or thrown into pits with throngs of hunting dogs or with similarly-tormented bears for public sport. Others had their jaws wired shut and were turned loose in the wild to die by thirst or, perhaps, to be killed by their own kind. Nobody knows for sure how many ani-mals died in America's wolfing campaigns all told. Some estimates suggest two million, others say more. What can be said is that while they once may have had their run of the top half of the planet, today, wild, free-ranging wolves generally survive only in the places modern humans do not.

Even in 1993—and even though a conviction for killing an endangered species carries a stiff sentence, as much
as a year in federal prison and a $100,000 fine—humans
were still believed to be the leading cause of death for
wolves in Wisconsin. Wydeven's calculations suggested as
much as 40 percent of the state's wolf population had died
in recent years—75 percent at the hands of humans and,
of that group, 40 percent as the specific result of gunshot
wounds.

Wydeven turned onto a stretch of two-lane asphalt highway, piled up speed, then leaned toward the middle of the
truck and hollered in short bursts over the roar of open
windows and passing cars. He was trying to explain the situation to me as he drove. We were traveling, he said,
through the territory of the McCarthy Lake pack in the
Chequamegon National Forest. The traps—two dozen,
sometimes three dozen sets were engaged at a single time—
were buried alongside a string of backroads in an area
shaped like an oblong trough, maybe thirty square miles
all told. The McCarthy Lake pack was known to occupy a
domain of about sixty square miles, about average for the
region. Up in the high Arctic, half a world away from Wisconsin, wolf pack territories can be as large as 5,000
square miles. So far, it had been twenty-one days since he
and Schultz plugged the first traps into the ground around
here and while there had been a few nibbles in those three
weeks, there had yet to be an outright bite.

"THIS IS THE THIRD YEAR WE'VE TRIED TRAPPING
IN HERE"—Wydeven shouted over wind and engine—"WE
HAVEN'T CAUGHT AN ANIMAL YET."

Due in part to the distance from his office in Park
Falls, neither Wydeven nor Schultz had ever been able to
track this particular pack regularly in winter. Snow allows
trackers to shadow wolf movements much more easily and
thoroughly, allowing them to better assess the runways,
travel habits and temperaments of the specific animals
they would be trying to collar a few months later. Wolves, it

could be argued, also lead more active and interesting lives in winter. While bears doze through the season in dens, wolves cast about comfortably under layers of insulating fur at temperatures as cold as forty below zero. Their characteristically wide feet, sometimes four or five inches across, have leathery pads that need remain only a few degrees above freezing. Thus equipped, wolves can scamper over the surface of deep snow while larger prey animals such as deer and elk—already weakened from months of meager winter energy reserves—punch and stumble up to their bellies in powder and ice because their hard, sharp hooves offer them footing there little better than carnival stilts. By and large, wolves eat better in the dead of winter than at any other time of the year. It's just as well, because they're also enduring the peak period of social stress within the pack. Throughout the northern hemisphere— from Siberia to Saudi Arabia, from Poland to Spain, from India to Italy, from South Carolina to the Yukon—wolves sort out pack hierarchy, "pair bond" and mate in January and February.

Based on a handful of tracking sessions and howling surveys that spring, Wydeven said they had reason to believe there were four wolves traveling in the McCarthy Lake pack at present—the alpha pair (the male and female leaders and usually the only breeders in a pack) and a couple of their offspring from previous spring litters. Four wolves in a pack seemed to be about average for Wisconsin, Wydeven said. In other places, the average pack size was usually about seven or eight wolves. The largest reliably-recorded pack was a group of thirty-six wolves that traveled South Central Alaska in 1967. Wydeven seemed to think Wisconsin's smaller average these days was related to local outbreaks of mange and parvo virus, diseases known to severely affect pup survival. In some cases, between 40 and 75 percent of each new litter died of the diseases. It was a situation Wydeven planned to watch closely for the next couple of years. Over the long haul, it could lead to serious problems.

In the meantime, Wydeven was beginning to run out of time and opportunity for collaring a McCarthy Lake wolf this summer. Schultz was due to start work on another trapping project in northeast Wisconsin in another seven days, and Wydeven himself, after investing the better part of a month in this one project, had other wolf packs and, for that matter, other whole species that required his attention.

Back at his office earlier that morning, Wydeven had shown me a map with oddly-shaped boundaries indicating known wolf pack territories throughout the state. They weren't arbitrary spaces. Wolf pack boundaries are sometimes described as *urine curtains*, a network of very deliberate and regularly maintained *scent marks* advertising the spaces each pack uses. In prime wolf habitat, pack territories often abut and, at times, overlap. Scent mark odors have been known to remain effective for as long as three weeks in the wild. Sniffing for the age and extent of a mark can tell wolves how recently another wolf or pack has passed by, how recently the area has been inspected for vulnerable prey and how likely it is that they will encounter an irritable neighbor anytime soon. Scent marks are also known to communicate to outsiders the breeding status of the alpha pair, whether they have bonded and whether there happens to be a vacancy in pack leadership currently.

Some of the circles, pie slices and islands on Wydeven's map of Wisconsin dipped west and north into Minnesota. When I asked about it, he said wolves basically couldn't care less about human political boundaries. Earlier that spring a female collared in Wisconsin crossed the state line and wandered all the way to the edge of a bee farm twenty miles from downtown St. Paul before she turned tail and scampered home in a series of short spurts. Breeding wolves have been known to take off on such long excursions before they settle down in the close quarters of a den to care for a litter of demanding pups day and night for eight to ten weeks.

When I asked Wydeven how many wolves were wearing radio collars in Wisconsin all together just then, he seemed to think about it for a moment before snapping the end of his pen at points on the map in blunt, precise sparks—

"We've got collared wolves as far as animals in packs *here, here,* ahh, *here, here,* ahh, *here,* ahh, *here,* down . . . *here,* we had one up here earlier but it disappeared recently . . . *here, here* and that'd be it."

I had tried to keep count on my fingers and asked, "So, about *nine?*"

"Nope," he answered. There were thirteen collars in nine packs.

All told that summer, Wisconsin was home to some forty eastern timber wolves in fourteen known packs. A state and federal wolf recovery plan first approved in 1978 and revised in January 1992 had set minimum population goals of eighty wolves for Wisconsin with another twenty next door on Michigan's upper peninsula. The plan's purpose was to promote a separate, viable range for the gray wolf subspecies known as *Canis lupus laycon* outside Minnesota, the only state in the lower forty-eight where wolves were listed as *threatened* rather than *endangered* because, by then, Minnesota's population had recovered to some 1,750 wolves. This smaller group of at least a hundred animals would serve as a kind of biological insurance policy in the event that disease or natural catastrophe decimated Minnesota's larger wolf population to the north. If all went according to plan, the revised goals might be reached as early as the year 2005—at a total estimated expense of $13.5 million—and the eastern timber wolf would be *delisted* from protected status throughout the Lake Superior region. If a separate population failed to take a firm hold in Wisconsin and Michigan, however, the same recovery plan directed the government to go looking for possible wolf habitat in Maine, New Hampshire and upstate New York where, in some cases, timber wolves had been absent for well more than a century.

Ron Schultz stood waiting for us beside the highway at the entrance to another unmarked road on the trapline. On first impression, Schultz looked to me more like a league bowler than an expert wolfer. He had a full beard and bushy hair, blond, red with some gray. He worked every day in a blue-checked flannel shirt, black jeans and elastic suspenders stretched over a ball-shaped belly right up front. He was by Wydeven's estimation, though, far and away the best wolf trapper on Wisconsin's state payroll. Of the more than seventy wolves collared in the state in fourteen years, Schultz had caught more than thirty. One of the first things he ever told me was he gave up deer hunting years earlier because it simply ceased to be a challenge.

"I had a Native American tell me once that a deer can *hear* a snowflake fall, a bear can *smell* a snowflake fall and an eagle can *see* a snowflake fall. Then he tells me a *wolf* can do all three."

Schultz seemed to watch me, then grinned.

"I have a lot of people that tell me I can't catch them. But I do."

Schultz drove a monster blue Chevy four-by-four pickup with knobby tires and a long, open bed with a black wooden box secured just behind the cab. The box looked to me like something simple and purposefully homemade, like something Schultz had crafted so as not to attract much attention in the region because this was the space where he kept his mysterious tangle of wolf traps and tools and nobody, I was told, absolutely nobody opened, nobody touched anything inside that box without gloves. Two traps pulled from the ground recently had been thrown in a corner of the bed near the tailgate. Each set weighed about eight pounds. They were a couple of mean, medieval-looking things, wrapped in mud, steel hooks and chains. These traps, I was told, would not be returned to service underground until Schultz had inspected all the parts carefully and boiled them in alder bark for half a day. The potion kept the trap parts lubricated, the story went, and helped mask the smell of the steel from the wolves.

While he and Wydeven bent over in tall grass and pulled on shin-high rubber boots, I moved my gear to the spot designated for observers in Schultz's truck. Along the way I noticed a growing swarm of dark flies buzzing around the back, orbiting like little airborne magnets, attracted and repelled by each other at once in mid-air, dozens of them drunk in a cloud of invisible reeks and effluvia rising out of a second, smaller box on the truck bed. It was Schultz's menagerie of potent scent baits, eight hand-labeled glass bottles and jars, an olfactory pleasure ground he had painstakingly engineered for compulsively curious canine noses: rotting deer liver, chicken parts, chunk beef, wolf urine, scat, capsules of ten-year-old wolf blood, and a couple of other bizarre-looking surprises I thought I might ask him to explain later. For now, though, I simply asked if dogs went crazy around this box. I said most dogs I knew would probably drag it over the tailgate, break everything open and roll around in whatever they didn't try to eat outright.

Schultz looked stern all of a sudden. Dogs, he said, have a propensity for falling into traps intended for wolves. Their noses are pulled to the same smells and their feet slip inside the same steel jaws. Yet, unlike wolves, dogs never calm down once they're caught; they just sit and bellow like car alarms until somebody shows up to let them out. By then, after that much racket, the local wolves knew to stay clear of the vicinity for a while. In another county, Schultz had caught one dog three times because the owner never heeded the posted warning notices and insisted on letting the animal run behind his pickup on the backroads. Schultz pointed into the trees where we were headed now and said, flatly—

"I guarantee, if you set a dog running loose in here, it would *never* make it out."

Several hundred yards later, Schultz mashed down on the brakes and killed the engine at a spot where the underbrush scraped both sides of the truck.

"I think I'm going to rebait this one," he said opening his door and lifting two bottles out of the back. He shook one like tabasco sauce as he walked. A moment later from the bush, he called—"We got *tracks.* Something went down there."

"Oh, *yeah?*" Wydeven said in the truck, reaching for his field notebook like it was his gunslinger's reflex.

"Coyote," Schultz said, apparently after a closer look. His voice telegraphed a shade of disappointment.

Sometimes called brush wolves or song dogs, coyotes are usually less than half the size of wolves around here, about thirty pounds each. They have a knack for exploiting the fringes of civilization, though, and are considered common all the way from Vermont to the suburbs of Los Angeles. Originally found only in isolated pockets of the arid West, the coyote's range expanded dramatically with human development and the decline of larger predators across the continent. They have taken over much of the range once held solely by wolves and, likewise, have become the subject of much the same scorn that wolves and their competitors used to have all to themselves. In some states, coyotes have been classified officially as vermin, a pest or agricultural nuisance open to private traps, poisons and pot shots all year long.

Wydeven leafed through open pages in the notebook on his lap. On charts and forms clamped tight under steel-ring binders, Wydeven kept a daily history of each trap on the line. For the record, he noted the coyote track. He noted the new scent bait.

"Urine and scat? Was that thirty-seven?"

There was a grunt or something like it as Schultz returned and rinsed his hands with water from a white plastic milk jug. He clambered back into the cab and the seatbelt buzzer howled for naught inside the dashboard as the engine kicked and Schultz wrenched the truck around to the opposite direction with a five-point, back-and-forth, rocking turn. The underbrush sprang back into place as the truck glided away.

"Any more along this road yet?" Wydeven asked, still flipping pages.

"That's it."

Later in the day, miles away, Schultz returned to the truck in a huff. He opened the door muttering—"That's not good"—to nobody in particular and hauled the truck down the road about thirty yards in the direction of the last trap he checked.

Schultz said wolves sometimes set off traps intentionally. Sometimes when a wolf knows there's a trap buried in the ground it gets excited and—"drops a load on it to let you know he was there." It was their way of alerting other wolves that there was danger in the ground right here, Schultz said. It was their way of protecting each other.

"But *this* one, he didn't know it was there because it scared the hell out of him."

Schultz said it looked as if this wolf was probably just trying to cover the smell of the scent with his own when the trap triggered and almost took a bite out of his behind. He pointed to signs of sudden disruption on the ground nearby where the wolf landed after it jumped.

"If they know a trap is there what they usually do is start *digging*."

It began to dawn on me in that moment that most times a trap was hidden in the ground a wolf knew it was there or, at the very least, sensed that there was something amiss about that parcel of earth. When I asked Schultz about it, he said I might be right.

"But ideally you catch them when they don't even know the ground is *hot*."

A good trapper, Schultz and other practitioners of the craft would come to explain later, has three basic types of trap sets in his arsenal.

An *open bait* appeals to a wolf's stomach. In the old days trappers used to stake out a deer or livestock carcass in an area littered with traps. Open baits are now illegal in Wisconsin because they tend to attract all manner of scavengers in the woods—raccoons, coyotes, feral cats and dogs, eagles and falcons. Sometimes when Schultz happened upon a road-killed deer he might still lug it to the general area of a trapline to attract wolves but not close enough to any specific traps to endanger smaller animals. If he wanted to put out meat as bait—like the chicken parts and rotting beef percolating in the back of his truck— he had to make sure it was covered well enough with rocks or logs not to attract raptorial birds at least. Open baits were Schultz's least-preferred, least-used trap set. He spoke of them with a degree of contempt, as if using them was beneath his true ability and standing as an expert wolfer.

A *scent bait* appeals to a wolf's curious, territorial nose. Wolf urine. Scat. The capsules of ten-year-old wolf blood. A drop or two would do because wolves are finicky about the upkeep of their boundary markers and *scent posts*. Schultz had to be careful to use only urine and scat collected from wolves in the same area so he wouldn't inad- vertently spread local diseases and parasites to packs all over the state. Scent baits were the most commonly-used sets on this particular trapline since, again, Schultz and Wydeven weren't as familiar as they wanted to be with this pack. Schultz seemed to use them only grudgingly. They were conspicuous by design. Wolves approached them knowing something was out of place, that something about this situation was already *hot*. Scent baits, Schultz explained in time, tended to fire a lot of blanks.

A *trail or trick set* relies on a wolf's inevitable absent- minded moments. There is no open meat or scent bait involved. A trapper buries a set in the ground based only on a hunch or informed guess that there was a high prob- ability a wolf will plant its foot in that precise spot during its travels. Trail sets were Schultz's favorite sets and, not surprisingly, the sets that required the most skill and tracking ability of a trapper. Schultz said he had nabbed most all his difficult wolves through the years with trail sets. They require, however, that he invest a lot of time and travel in the backwoods to learn a particular wolf's stride, rhythms and idiosyncrasies, to figure out what kind of terrain that wolf likes to feel under its feet and, essentially, to crawl inside that wolf's head. You could follow a wolf closely for weeks, sometimes months, Schultz said, before you found the perfect spot to lay a trail set that stood a chance of catching it. Unfortunately, he didn't have that kind of time left this year to get to know the McCarthy Lake pack. He was approaching these wolves almost like a complete stranger. After twenty-one days, though, it seemed to me that Schultz and this particular wolf had begun to strike up something of an acquaintance.

"He must have been captured before or caught in a coyote trap because he goes all over," Schultz said, his eyes following a trail on the ground that may as well have been left by a ghost. He pointed to an indentation in the mud a few steps away.

"I've got another trap right *there* but I don't think it's going to work."

The ground Schultz was watching was wet and packed from rain the night before. Schultz said it looked like that second trap was triggered, too, but didn't close. Sometimes when that happened Schultz put a new trap right back into the same hole as a suspected misfire. Sometimes he filled the hole with dirt and sank a new trap a couple feet away. It just depended on how smart he thought the wolf was. This one seemed to be kindling respect because Schultz resolved to replace the trap outright.

"I don't want to miss him again to something like *that*."

Schultz said once, two years earlier, it took him sixty-nine days to catch an ornery wolf he called Bo. Known also as #128M in Wydeven's old field notebooks, Bo had since become the founding male of the Bootjack Lake pack about fifty miles to the southwest in Price and Oneida counties.

"Now, Bo was *smart*. He would just play tricks with me. It was just between him and me. I would go out there and it wouldn't be unusual to have five of my traps dug up. Didn't even scare him."

Schultz's attention seemed to drift back to the matter at hand. Wolf tracks tell stories if you know how to read them. Each foot print, in a sense, serves as a preserved syllable. Wolves can bound in single strides as great as sixteen feet. They can sprint for as long as twenty minutes at speeds of upwards of forty-five miles an hour. They can trot tirelessly for hours at speeds between five and ten miles an hour. It's not at all unusual for wolves to cover more than forty-five miles in a single day or, for that matter, more than 200 miles at a stretch.

All canines are said to be more elegantly engineered for traveling than any other family of meat eaters. They step on four toes with a fifth toe, or *vestigial dew claw*, which could be said to correspond to the human thumb, positioned well above the ground on the front foot and which is entirely absent from the hind foot. Each resulting wolf track usually includes those first four toes, sometimes with a claw tip dipping off the front of each, along with a central *interdigital pad* which, in effect, corresponds to the heel of our palm. Sometimes in deep, detailed wolf tracks left in mud slight webbing stands out between the toes. Unlike humans, though, the wolf's front feet are significantly larger than the back since most of its weight is carried directly above in its chest and head and since, as car designers have found, front-wheel drive offers distinct advantages in the way of power, traction and maneuverability.

One of the first lessons of wildlife tracking phraseology is that only bipeds such as ourselves actually *run*. Four-legged creatures, which have to master movement without kicking and stepping all over themselves, maneuver through a complicated variety of what we call *gaits*— beginning with basic walks, trots and gallops, and continuing with more sophisticated patterns of jumps, hops, bounds, lopes, canters, ambles and crawls. What wild animals are not generally known to do, however, is *pace*, a term applied to a particular gait in which both the front and back leg of the same side of the body move together at the same moment, as some thoroughbred horses are trained to do. When people try to walk this way consciously, with right and left arms swinging in unison with the leg of the same side, they usually come off teetering like toy soldiers. Slow, small and burly animals with wide bodies and short legs, such as raccoons, may be the only common exceptions for the absence of pacing in the wild. A wolf's carriage, by contrast, is compact. Its forelimbs are pressed into a narrow chest with the elbows turned slightly inward and the paws turned slightly outward. This rigging allows wolves' limbs, fore and aft, to swing along the same narrow line which—like tire treads on speedway straightaways—makes traveling faster, more efficient and, again, easier through snow. It's not at all unusual for wolves to place their hind feet atop the exact spot used by its front feet, and when that happens a tracker can conclude that the animal was probably moving at a steady pace at that moment—maybe fast, maybe slow, but definitely steady.

Distance between front and hind tracks indicates a change of speed. If the smaller hind foot steps beyond the larger track of the front the animal was probably extending itself and accelerating. If the hind foot falls behind the track of the front, in turn, a tracker could conclude that the animal was putting on the brakes and slowing down. An indication of higher speed can also manifest itself in signs that the animal's straddle, or the distance between left and right tracks, has gotten narrower. Competitive runners move much the same way, with their feet falling on a narrow line at high speed rather than thrown wide apart like a football lineman. Wolves are known for moving in particularly precise and directed lines as opposed to domestic dogs, for instance, which tend to leave tracks that wander more haphazardly.

Sorting out the placement of individual tracks into the context of complete strides, or *intergroups*, can help a tracker begin to make guesses about what was actually going through a wolf's mind at that moment. The placement of the front feet in relationship to the wolf's general line of travel, for example, can be an indication of what direction the wolf was looking. If the front feet are swung to the right of the general center line, tacking briefly like a sailboat, it was probably looking to the right. Watching carefully for such clues helps trackers draw conclusions about a particular wolf's approach to its environment—if it bolts through the edges of developed areas, if it slows down to consider more carefully the banks of waterways populated with beaver, or if it treats some spots along its regular travels more casually, almost indifferently.

Those were the very points that Schultz prospected for like gold, the points at which a wolf's guard strayed and it might be induced to trip into one of his traps. So far, though, Schultz had been able to deduce only that this particular wolf had a habit of creeping up on a trap and then carefully retreating.

"So what I'm going to do is sink another one right about—*here*." Schultz demonstrated how a wolf might approach a suspected trap and then back into another one.

"*Trick* him," Schultz said. "It comes down to *one-on-one* most times."

Schultz found and pressed the fat end of a fallen tree branch against the mud that had clogged the trap he suspected of triggering but not closing and—too fast for my eyes to follow—steel jaws sprang into the wood. It sounded to me like a meat cleaver biting deep into a butcher's block and as I said so, Schultz casually set about extracting the limb from the clenched works. I asked Schultz if anyone had ever calculated how many pounds per square inch whipped off those machines. Wolf jaws, I had read, exert as much as 1,500 pounds of pressure per square inch, enough to crush open moose bones. Human jaws, by comparison, chomp down at a paltry twenty-five pounds. Schultz kept working and said he had never calibrated the exact bite of his traps, not that it didn't matter.

"I weaken the strength," he said, pulling the hook and steel chain out of the hole. I heard sucking sounds as the mud choked it up. "We're constantly working on new traps.

These actually are Minnesota jaws. They're patented by the Fish and Wildlife Service. This pan system is made in Pennsylvania. But basically it's the same Newhouse trap from the old days.

"Some of the modifications I've made, see *here*, I went to a half-inch drag instead of the three-eighths." This, I gathered, meant he had installed a heavier chain between the trap and its trailing steel hook. "Then I put a spring on *here*"—he tugged a coil spring between a loop in the chain and the trap frame—"so that when they pull, it's not a sudden *jerk*. Right now we're working on a new type of a snare system that'll be better yet."

Metal clinked against metal as Schultz coiled the chain around the mechanism like a ball of yarn and dropped the whole heavy mess into the truck bed.

"I'm not a trapper. I don't want to *hurt* the animals."

At first, watching Schultz sink a new trap in the ground is like watching a Sunday gardener fidget quietly on his knees. There are sounds of birds announcing their territories in the distance, a trowel piercing soil and then, sometimes, fierce hammering like shots of a pneumatic jack chewing through a city sidewalk. The least clandestine task of Schultz's job is clearing a hole for each trap about ten inches across and six inches deep. Rock and debris have to be cleared from the space and brute force is sometimes the best available means.

A blunt-end hook goes first into the bottom of the hole. It isn't expected to hold a permanent grip like a cemented fence post. Wolves are too strong for trappers to expect any quick staking job to hold very long. The idea is for a wolf to haul all eight pounds of jaws, chain and hook straight out of the ground and then let it snag itself somewhere in the brush nearby. It's better to let the animal have some control over its movements right after the big surprise, Schultz said, better to let it hobble safely into the underbrush where it could feel more secure than if it were left exposed by the side of a road for hours, maybe a whole night, where poachers and rival predators could spot it and do it in.

When Schultz pounds the hook into the hole, it too is heavy and hard, like he's smashing at a blacksmith's anvil. The hook needs to be solid, flat and level in the bottom because everything that really matters rests on top of it.

Schultz then stands, straddles the device he has laid out on the ground next to the hole and clamps the heels of his boots down on two steel leaf springs. The ends of each spring are bent back toward one another like a compressed *V* with holes in the ends fitted around the sides of the jaws. When the trap goes off, those springs slide up the jaws and force them closed around a wolf's leg. While the springs are still pinned down under Schultz's weight, though, the jaws are lazy, as limp, loose and heavy as a mouth shot full of novocaine. Schultz sets the triggering mechanism, a round pan that looks like a flattened mixing spoon, by working his fingers forcefully in the works between his feet. As soon as the trigger holds and he steps off the springs, though, his every movement becomes more delicate, like he's needling a house of cards. Schultz makes fine adjustments to a screen designed to keep dirt from falling under the pan, leaving ample room for the pan to drop when a wolf steps on it. There's a coil spring under the pan, too, so the trigger resists and is less likely to be tripped by smaller animals. A critter has to weigh at least twenty-eight pounds to get the full attention of one of Schultz's traps. A human foot is too broad and long to fit into a wolf trap, unless one happens to be walking tip-toe in precisely the wrong spot.

Next, the compressed springs are folded on their axes at right angles back against the trap frame to save space. Schultz coils the chain carefully above the hook at the bottom of the hole and places the trap on top. Good trappers are careful to align their sets according to the surrounding terrain so an animal is likely to step into it straight. They want the trap to close along the width of a wolf's leg bone so it fits like a wrist watch with the clock works facing up or down rather than biting into an edge. Modern catch-and-release traps are engineered to leave a bit of open space between closed jaws and with rows of widely-set flat prongs that look something like square teeth carved into a Halloween jack-o-lantern. They are designed to keep a firm grip so a wolf can't wiggle and saw off its own leg after a few hours of persistent struggle. These modern prongs sometimes cause a small puncture wound, Schultz said, but there is less pain, less damage to the wolf overall than with old-fashioned pointed teeth or no teeth at all. They may leave a minor cut that will heal quickly, like a kid's scraped knee, Schultz said, except wolves are no strangers to blood, either their own or what comes out of the things they eat.

Once the trap is in the ground Schultz takes up a wooden frame with a wide-gauge screen and sifts dirt back into the hole like baker's flour. He pats the pile down gently with the back of his gloved fingers then goes looking for surface dirt of matching grade and color nearby. He uses the trowel blade to lift just the very top grains that are bleached by the sun and sprinkles them over the disturbed area to hide things convincingly.

He then looks things over one last time and considers how much time the operation has taken. If it was longer than five or six minutes, Schultz said, he may as well go ahead and pull the thing out of the ground there and then because there's probably so much human scent left in the area no wolf in its right mind will ever come near it.

"You gonna pull *seven, eight, nine* there?" Wydeven called, standing over his field book laid open on the hood of the truck.

The numbers correspond to the order and placement of traps on the line. Wydeven needed to consult the book sometimes to remember their names. Schultz seemed to have them all memorized.

Schultz considered Wydeven's question at length, apparently weighing past strategies against what he had learned recently, then replied, in a word—"*Yeah.*"

"How about *one* and *two*?"

"I don't know. I kinda liked them."

Schultz slipped on a white surgical glove and tore open the plastic wrap around a pound of hamburger he had left to rot in the truck bed for a few days. He was finally resorting to open bait and he didn't look too thrilled about it. He hid a pinch under a rock about fourteen inches from the center of the covered hole so when a wolf stepped close to sniff the bait the trap would close around its foot.

"Big Mac here was a real good hitter for years. Then they got kind of *wise* to it."

Schultz said a colleague once called him from Minnesota to ask if he was really using fast-food sandwiches as bait on his traplines. The guy wanted to know if there was something special about the restaurant meat that attracts wolves.

Schultz said—"Nah. Doesn't have to be *green.*"

In the event that Schultz and Wydeven actually find a wolf in one of their traps there is a processing kit, another unopened box in the truck that looks like a jumbo tackle box any pack-rat fisherman would love, with compartments for three kinds of tranquilizers, reversal drugs, penicillin, vaccines, vials for collecting blood, tapes and measures, a thermometer, vials for collecting ectoparasites, a scale to weigh the animal, rubber gloves and, certainly, the radio collar and electronic gear to test the transmitter. Schultz said a captured wolf is usually docile and quiet as they approach it in the underbrush, that maybe it knows enough about the situation and people by then to realize it faces overwhelming odds and it may as well submit calmly to whatever comes next.

What trapped wolves usually face first from these two these days is the ginger application of a jab stick, a tranquilizer syringe at the end of a long pole, a technique I once heard them describe, jokingly, as the "Marlon Perkins method." The drug takes effect after about fifteen minutes and usually lasts a couple of hours. Throughout that time the wolf's body temperature is monitored constantly, usually with a rectal thermometer. Wolves don't sweat, they pant to dissipate excess heat and since they can't pant very well while they're tranquilized and since overheating can cause lasting brain damage, the biologists always have to be ready to cool it down with soaking water and glucose injections. The tranquillizer itself is usually a disassociative drug, a combination of chemicals that scramble the perceptions, messages and instructions going to and from the brain. In humans, such drugs have the effect of a hallucination or a bad dream. The wolf's eyes remain wide open during processing, taking everything in, as if in a trance, so the biologists often cover and protect them and speak softly, too, to keep the animal calmer and, in effect, cooler.

Next, the wolf is weighed with a hanging scale. Born blind to the world at about a pound each, wolves can weigh as much as seventy-five pounds by the time they're five months old. Around Wisconsin, some adult wolves have been known to weigh as much as a hundred pounds but usually, Schultz said, they measure out between sixty and ninety pounds, with males larger than females. As with most wild mammals, wolves gradually get larger the further north they live. Scientists have decided it has something to do with the efficiency of surface area in maintaining body temperature through the colder winters of northern climates, that it's easier for larger animals to keep their body mass warm with their proportion of skin and fur than smaller creatures.

The biologists then take blood samples, search for evidence of parasites and disease, examine the wolf's teeth to estimate its age and collect other data related to their specific study and local purpose. In other research and recovery programs of late, biologists have begun stitching button-sized radioactive chips under a wolf's skin, too, to shed trace elements through its body and help them better track and distinguish the scat of individual wolves.

If the collar itself is fitted properly, Schultz said he should be able to slip the four fingers of a flattened palm between the collar and the wolf's neck. On young wolves biologists are known to bolt the collar together a size or two larger and then wrap foam rubber around the inside so the wolf can still grow into it without choking before the extra padding falls away.

All told, Schultz said, it usually takes an hour or so to process a captured wolf from start to finish. Afterward, they make a practice of watching from a short distance for as long as it takes the animal to clear its head and stagger off to safety.

With that remaining down time, they usually check and recheck the collar's radio transmitter and settings. The frequencies themselves are kept secret to make it harder for poachers to tune in and track down collared wolves. For similar reasons of secrecy, biologists using telemetry gear and two-way radios to communicate in the field are instructed not to actually utter the word *Wolf* over open airwaves. Instead, they use code words like *Whiskey, Big Al* or *The Critter*, which could mean a deer, bear, badger, beaver, lynx, or any other manner of fauna that eavesdropping locals are accustomed to government biologists collaring and following around the woods.

Basic collar units—versions of which have been used for more than thirty years to study creatures as diverse as antelope and elephants, frogs and fish—weigh about 500 grams, or a little less than a pound, and emit a continuous series of plinks that a receiver translates into sounds something like the flat, electronic inflections of early video games. Experienced trackers can interpret the signals for indications of a wolf's distance and activity—if it is *down* and resting, for instance, or *up* and busy going about its daily business. Reception is line-of-sight, as with all AM radio waves, and signals can be lost if a subject passes through a low-lying hollow, like a car driving through a highway tunnel. In more mountainous regions, trackers also have to contend with frequency bounce, being careful to confirm that the signal is coming directly to the antenna from the collar and not reflecting off, say, a sheer cliff face. Tracking with basic collars, in a sense then, is like a game of high-tech hide-and-seek, where all study information is collected, managed and interpreted on the receiving end.

A new generation of much more sophisticated *capture collars* had been developed in the previous decade, however, specifically with wolf research and recovery in mind. They feature miniaturized, on-board computers that can receive coded instructions from a remote-control field panel. They can switch off temporarily to conserve batteries. They can monitor a subject's head movements with mercury-switch sensors. They can sort and store accumulated data with memory chips and manage the flow of information back to base units with state-of-the-art communications circuitry. They also, most significantly, come equipped with automated firing mechanisms in two tranquilizer dart chambers that look almost like a pair of newfangled saddlehorns sprouting off the top of the collar. Packed with just a touch of anti-freeze, the darts are aimed directly at the thick muscles on either side of a wolf's spine. They are also designed to break off and fall out if, for some reason, they fail to take effect. Wydeven said that researchers learned during the testing phase not to initiate a *knock down*, however, if there was any hint of water in the immediate area. One Wisconsin test subject apparently fell with its nose plunged into a puddle only a few inches deep and drowned before Wydeven's team could get to it. Capture collars are otherwise becoming a staple of many wolf management plans across the country, particularly in situations where local farmers and ranchers want assurance that wolves can be readily controlled if there is trouble with their livestock. They offer a much more realistic and reliable means of recatching, studying and managing individual wolves than sending trappers after them with leg-hold traps for a second, third or fourth time. Wolves, as Schultz had already mentioned, tend to get harder to catch after they have been caught a first time.

As it was, three weeks into the third consecutive June of trapping around here, he and Wydeven were still trying to catch even their first wolf from the McCarthy Lake pack. Near the end of my first day there, though, I saw Schultz spot something, stop short and get out of his truck in a hurry to scour the surface of the ground for clues.

"You see the mistake this guy makes here. He did this one other time a week ago." Schultz pointed and pantomimed wolf movements around nearby rocks and plants and grades of dirt.

"See what he did? He went up *there* and walked up through *there* and went down. He knows there's a trap there but what he's doing here is he's stepping *here* investigating it. Same thing he did the other day.

"If I can find where he's coming down that bank I can put a trail set right there and rig it so he has to step over something and he'll step right into the trap."

So Schultz seemed to think he finally had this wolf's number.

"I *dare* him to do it again."

Maybe the wolf heard him. I was riding in the truck cab beside Schultz the next morning as we coasted to a stop back at the very same spot. I could almost make out the tire tracks we left driving away the day before.

Schultz looked out the window and he said—"*Ope.*"

Wydeven heard, stood straight up in truck bed in back, looked down and said—"*Hoooah.*"

Everybody stared at a hole in the ground. Keys turned counter-clockwise in the ignition, Schultz's door opened and Wydeven dropped off the back. The two trained biologists conferred over the dirt and Schultz returned, shaking his head.

"He pulled it right out of there."

"You think it's the same wolf again?" Wydeven called from the edge of the hole.

"I don't know. I *hope* not." Schultz sounded like he was trying not to sound annoyed in front of company.

"That was a good release, too, there was nothing wrong with that one. There's no hair or nothing."

Wydeven went to work implementing their next strategy. They had decided to sink a new trap six inches from the first.

"Leave the hole?" Wydeven asked.

"Nope. Make the hole smooth like there's a trap there."

If the same wolf came back it might be lulled into overconfidence about the location of the old trap and step into a new one. There was silence for a moment as Schultz and I listened to Wydeven's tools work the dirt. Schultz leaned against the truck bed and watched.

"Well, he's not as bad as Bo yet. If it was him we'd come down here and *every* trap would have been out. This one at least jumps when the trap goes off. Bo never did jump. He knew what he was doing."

Schultz described how Bo would inch toward each trap, claw carefully around the edges until he could pull it clean out of the ground, the trigger and jaws still set in place, still ready to bite. Schultz said he took it to be Bo's form of personal insult.

"The first few times that happens you think, well, it was just an accident. But then after you go through it four traps in a row like that you *know* it's no accident."

Schultz told me he liked to trade stories with hunters, farmers and ranchers he meets in his travels on the job.

There was, he said, this one deer hunter in Michigan's Upper Peninsula—

"I still think he considers himself *anti-wolf.* But he saw a wolf once when he was on a deer stand. He was *so* excited. He told me he'll never forget that for as long as he lives. He said it just kind of *slithered* through the woods. I think it stuck in his mind more seeing that wolf than all the bucks he got through the years. It's like fishing. You always remember the ones that get away. But the ones you *catch*, they always just kind of fade away."

Another hunter once told Schultz there was a big buck out in the woods that he wanted for his freezer and he just knew the wolves got to that buck. Just knew it—

"I asked him if that made him mad and he said, *sure, since he only gets to hunt nine days out of the year*. So I said, '*What if I told you I know the hunter who shot that buck. Would you be mad at him?*' And he looks at me and thinks about it and says, '*Prob'ly.*'"

Then there was the time that a radio collar tracking van pulled into a gas station a bit farther south in the state—

"This kid, maybe eighteen-, nineteen-years-old comes out and asks what we're doing. So we said we were looking for wolves, that we heard there were some down here.

"He says, '*Oh yeah. Sure, there's quite a few.*'

"So we say, '*How many are there?*' We had him going, see.

"And he says, '*Twenty-six, at least.*' We had about four wolves in the area, maybe five.

"Anyway, we said, '*Well, how did they get there?*' You know, we're sure we're going to hear it from this guy.

"So he says, '*Oh, you don't know about that?*'

"And I say, '*No. We don't know. Tell us.*'

"He said, '*They were planted. It's a long story, but I'll tell you real fast. They came in at night. They had crates and parachutes and they dropped them wolves out of planes and when them crates hit the ground they broke and the wolves come out.*'

"So we say, '*Why did they do that? Who did it?*'

"And he says, '*Oh, yeah, sure. The paper companies did it.*'

"So we ask, '*Why did the paper companies do it?*'

"And he says, '*Oh, the deer eat all the little trees that the paper company plants. So they drop all these wolves off so they eat the deer so the trees can grow.*'"

"You run into all kinds," Wydeven told me riding slow in his Bronco that first day.

"Some just think of wolves as symbols of wilderness and wild areas. Then there are some who have this mind set just on wolves. They have these mystical attitudes about wolves. They don't necessarily have strong environmental attitudes or concerns. They're just interested in wolves.

"It's almost as if there are wolf *groupies* out there now. It's like the wolf has become a super animal that can't do any harm. It can't do anything bad. We can't ever kill a wolf under any circumstances. For some people it's like wolves are the next best thing to God anymore."

Wydeven smiled and said he owns quite a few wolf T-shirts himself. Some were presents. Some he bought.

"But if it's just me, I like to see the wolf used as a kind of guide for teaching people about broader environmental concerns, about the whole ecosystem and biodiversity, things that, in the long run, are more important than wolves by themselves.

"Wolves show us some of our wildest lands. An area that can support wolves is probably as near a complete ecosystem as you're likely to make. So if we're able to maintain healthy wolf populations in managed ecosystems that tells me we've gone a long ways as far as learning how to live with the land.

"I think wilderness preservation is a good idea and we should be preserving the environment whenever it's possible. But I don't think the way that we're going to maintain and manage for biodiversity is by creating more and more wilderness set-aside areas. We have to learn how to manage the lands we already have."

Late in the afternoon of my third day on the trapline, Schultz inspected the soft ground around a downed pine blocking what used to be a narrow road through the underbrush. He pointed to where a wolf had walked past the top of the tree to get around.

"*Look*, he went through *there*." His expression said this was just the spot he had been hoping to find for more than three weeks.

"Made another little mistake. All we've got to do now is *outsmart* the guy."

It became a trail set like previous trail sets except this time Schultz didn't say a word to either Wydeven or me while he was working. Once the trap was in the ground and the surface was almost smoothed over Schultz went looking for special effects. He came back with three small woody plants and injected them with his trowel into the dirt above and around the trap.

Wydeven noted the technique in his notebook and said—"In a previous life, Ron was a landscape architect."

This became trap number forty-two in Wydeven's book. Thirty-one traps were still in service on the line after twenty-three days. Schultz was whispering by the time he finished. I assumed he was talking to the wolf. When he returned to the truck he said you have to think like a wolf sometimes to catch one, that some things about this job go beyond science into intuition. Then he said—

"What we really *need* is a hidden camera over there so we can watch everything that's going on."

Schultz didn't bait the trap but he did sprinkle a special concoction of smells throughout the area, including deer scent, to help mask presence of three men and a truck.

"I try to pick the scents that are natural in the woods around here. Coyote and beaver. In fact, there's a beaver lodge right there."

"Was it a trail set you finally caught Bo on?" Wydeven asked, closing his book.

"Yeah. Actually, what Bo did before that is he *rolled* right through one of my trail sets to set it off and then he got up on the other side and walked away."

Schultz climbed back into the cab and looked the scene over one last time before he triggered the engine and backed away. He started nodding and threw a glance toward me.

"A couple days and we'll *have* this guy."

A while later on the third day I was riding in the truck cab alone with Schultz on a quiet road through dense pine. Schultz and Wydeven had been gracious toward me but it was already late afternoon and, unlike the two previous days, I hadn't yet been invited to meet them again before work the next morning. It was clear to me that I had been slowing them down in these last few days they had with the McCarthy Lake pack this year. It was also long since clear to everyone that I wasn't going to be able to watch them collar and process a wolf during this visit.

For some reason, though, it didn't bother me. Maybe after three days with them on the trapline I was just beginning to be able to read a few of the stories on my own and, maybe, I felt that was enough for me for now.

Time passed and I asked Schultz how often he got to see a wolf moving free in the wild.

"Every year usually. This year I haven't yet."

He told me about an evening the previous summer when he went out on a howling survey with his wife and young son, how they came upon four small wolves— probably that season's litter of pups—walking down a logging road with a larger wolf that looked to be a subordinate member in the pack's hierarchy. Subordinate wolves usually carry their tails parallel to the ground behind them, sometimes lower depending on their rank. Pack leaders, the alpha male and female, brandish their tails high, sometimes as close to perpendicular as a wolf tail can get. Schultz told me how he instructed his wife and son to get down in low profile and how he started whining and squealing at the adult in the falling light.

"It came running up to me and it showed aggression. It stopped right by us. It was running, and it stopped and growled and showed its teeth. And I would growl. Then an alpha animal came from our left and circled us. All the while, this alpha kept going around us. Then the pups came out on a hill, a couple of them looking right at us.

"For about thirty-five, forty minutes—until the mosquitoes were so thick around us we couldn't see—we carried on an aggression. I would whine and howl. Then we'd all howl and they would howl right with us. It was like we were another pack intruding on their territory. We weren't quite *wolfy* enough to approach, but we weren't *not* wolfy enough to leave us alone.

"When we sort of snuck out of there it was getting dark. The animals were still there and this subordinate was half-circling us and growling and just carrying on."

That was just last year, Schultz said again.

"So that made my whole ten years of wolf work all worthwhile."

The terrain changed and the road started to rumble loud under the wheels again but Schultz's eyes were still fixed and reflective. The air that night was just black with mosquitoes, he said. They had to leave.

Schultz was quiet then for miles. I imagined we were both lingering in the same moment, on the image of Schultz with his family, Carol and Christopher, all of them crouching and growling and howling and trading insults of gibberish and tone with a corresponding family of wolves, circling alphas and subordinates with four pups sitting safely away on a hill, watching.

I asked Schultz what it felt like to finally bag Bo.

"Oh, I was real happy. But he had mange real bad. So I felt both kind of happy and sad because of the shape he was in. He didn't have much hair left and I didn't think he would live. But he did.

"Right now he's got a family. He had a family last year, too. Two pups. It's too early to say about this year.

"But you get that good feeling and then that not so good feeling, I guess. You feel good you outsmart them but then you've caught them, you know? It's not so bad when you release them again.

"I guess I'm not a *true* trapper. I could never have done anything to them after I've caught them."

I ran across Wydeven again Saturday morning, three days later, in Ely, Minnesota, 250 miles north and west of the McCarthy Lake pack territory, fifteen miles from the border with Canada, in the seat of two million acres of designated wilderness area combined in the Boundary Waters Canoe Area and Quetico Provincial Park. Historically, the labyrinth of forest, water and farms in Minnesota's northeastern tip was the only spot in the continental U.S. where wolves were never fully cast out of their native range. It was where Sigurd Olson began the first scientific study of wolves more than fifty years ago and it was where, this weekend, more than 500 people piled onto a hill overlooking highway 169 for the official opening of Ely's brand new International Wolf Center.

It had once been the site of the Voyageur Visitor Center, a state and federal facility where canoers and campers come for backcountry permits. It was now a $3 million, 16,000 square foot lodge with knotty-pine walls, exposed beams, glass skylights and a freestanding stone chimney in the lobby. There was a 1.5-acre enclosure outside for a resident pack of four hand-raised, captive wolves—three females and a male, named MacKenzie, Kiana, Lakota and Lucas, respectively—who had just turned seven weeks old and weighed about twenty-pounds each. Inside, ample space had been set aside as the permanent home for a sixty-ton, 6,000 square foot "Wolves and Humans" exhibit amassed by the Science Museum of Minnesota ten years earlier for a tour of twenty-one cities with 2.5 million total viewers—from Anchorage, Miami, Boston and Honolulu to Yellowstone National Park, the National Geographic Explorer Hall in Washington, D.C. and the American Museum of Natural History in New York City. By that Saturday, the Wolf Center counted more than 5,000 dues-paying members from every U.S. state and twenty-two countries, all of whom were invited to attend the grand opening.

For those who could make it, there were world pre-miere screenings of "In the Company of Wolves," a docu-mentary produced by and starring the actor Timothy Dalton for the public television series *Nature*. There were windy speeches by politicians and dignitaries, raffles for howling trips with visiting scientists, silent auctions, a fish fry and children's presentations by Nancy Gibson, a natu-ralist from the public television show, *Newton's Apple*. Gib-son was dressed for the occasion in a long cape just like Little Red Riding Hood. Now and again there were lectures, too, by prominent wolf biologists. Three had flown in from Italy, Poland and the former Soviet Union at the invitation of L. David Mech, widely-considered to be the presiding, so-called alpha male among wolf researchers in North America. During one of the breaks, I overheard Mech, quite earnest, bearded and balding, struggling to communicate through an interpreter with Dimitri Bibikov, his white-haired Russian contemporary.

"Yes, *yes*, I understand," Mech said, huddled close to the man in the chair beside him, their knees almost touch-ing. "When you kill so many wolves, the ones that survive are very *clever*."

All weekend, Mech was hailed in speeches, receptions and casual conversation as, perhaps, the true founder of Ely's new wolf center. He had been among the first, after all, to suggest in 1972 that the wolf in Minnesota could someday become what Old Faithful is to Yellowstone. On Monday morning, the day after the celebrations closed and most of the guests had left town, the *Ely Echo* concurred. An editorial that appeared under the headline, "Who'da Thunk It?" said, among other things—

> It takes some mental adjustment to realize much of this is pretty awesome stuff to city folk. . . . There is no question but what Ely is sitting on some sort of an economic bonanza regarding the wolves and the Wolf Center.

Early that Saturday in Ely, though, while the assembly was still waiting outside for Minnesota Governor Arne

Carlson to arrive with official scissors to cut open a yellow-plastic ribbon draped across the entrance, I found myself inching through a tide to shake hands again with Wisconsin's Adrian P. Wydeven. He was all cleaned up and combed, wearing street clothes for the first time since I had known him—a brown corduroy jacket and a pressed white dress shirt with an open collar. He had his arms crossed in front of him and he seemed to smile and swagger a bit against bystanders' shoulders. He told me what had happened the day before, the last scheduled day of operation this year for the trapline down in the McCarthy Lake pack territory.

"Caught a wolf," Wydeven said. "Big yearling male, about eighty pounds."

Old Faithful

IN JULY, FOUR WEEKS AND FOUR STATES FARTHER WEST, I FOUND myself at odds with another small mob, this time entering an auditorium at the Old Faithful Visitor Center in the most famous and visited corner of Yellowstone National Park. It was a room without many right angles, with a ceiling that sloped from low in back to high up front where a rear-projection slide-show screen was framed into the loftiest wall. Below and back a few strides were fifty or so cushioned, orange vinyl chairs set in five or six long, fixed rows and, as it happened that evening, a slightly greater number of people vying to find places in them. Moments before eight o'clock, though, perhaps as a signal to strike a final seating compromise, a man wearing a park ranger uniform, a thin beard and glasses appeared with a luxurious gray wolf pelt draped over one arm. He stepped through the rows and encouraged the children he met to touch it, to stroke the long, soft fur. He reassured them, time and again, *it won't bite.*

"*Welcome* to Yellowstone National Park on a very beautiful summer's day," he said looking directly into a few faces, minutes later. As he gave his name, I remembered noticing a tag pinned to his shirt that said, *Frank Yochim.*

The ranger drew out a firm pause, perhaps to command greater attention, before adding, "It's *cool* today."

Nods came back, as if to reply—*Why yes, Ranger Frank, it does seem cool for July.* Yochim's voice was calm and melodic, a tenor shaping phrases like an elementary school teacher. About half his audience was either very young or very old, small children and senior citizens, with the remainder consisting of teenagers and adults who attended to them. Citing this as his sixth summer as a seasonal ranger in Yellowstone—during his winters off he said he usually taught Nordic skiing up in Big Sky, Montana—Yochim launched into reminders about bear-country restrictions listed in the park newspaper, about the junior ranger program, upcoming guided tours and campfire talks. He warned his listeners to keep safe distance from the park buffalo. As the largest land mammal in North America, each can weigh as much as 2,000 pounds.

"If you're closer than about thirty feet to a bison—well, legally about twenty-five yards, which equates to seventy-five feet—you're in that bison's *personal* space. And since about 1968, we have had more injuries per year caused by bison than any other animal in Yellowstone. People think they're *tame* when they're not."

Yochim joked about potholes in the park's roadways that may be old enough to earn historic designation. He told drivers the average speed in Yellowstone was about thirty miles an hour, that they should give themselves plenty of time to make their destinations.

"If you see an animal, by all means, pull over and enjoy and view that animal. You may not see it again. But, like I said, *pull* over. *Don't*—and we get this every summer—*don't* leave your car with engine running and all four doors open in the middle of the road. That's always an entertaining sight for the rangers.

"One final word about driving. If you see a bicyclist, remember, they've got to dodge the potholes too. So *please*, give them plenty of room. Especially if you're driving a large RV with overhanging mirrors. We lost a person just yesterday—not on a bike but standing on the side of the road—when she was hit by one of those mirrors. So *do* be careful."

Yochim walked over to a small boy in the front row with a junior ranger patch on his jacket and began to quiz him on the spot, right there, right then in front of all those other kids, parents and strangers.

"What's the cardinal rule of boardwalks?"

The boy squirmed and replied, quietly—"Stay on them."

"Did you hear that?" Yochim asked the audience. "He said, '*Stay on them.*'"

Yochim faced the boy again. "Why do I want to stay on boardwalks?"

"Because, *uhmmm*," the boy said. "You want—holes in the ground, *uhmmm*, under you, that you can't see, from the cracks, in the area."

Yochim seemed to suppress a grin as he translated for the room.

"He says the ground in the thermal areas can be *very* thin, *deceivingly* thin, under which there might be boiling water. And it is possible for you to fall through, to break through that crust and fall through."

Yochim nodded approvingly at the boy and there was a smattering of applause nearby. He then described second-and third-degree burns, prolonged medical treatment and painful skin grafts.

"We *do* get thermal burns every year in Yellowstone. We've had several already this year. Yellowstone is a wild and beautiful place. But it's also a *dangerous* place."

A white-haired woman seated near the center of one of the middle rows tossed up a hand then. She must have grown tired of all the niceties, all of the ranger's cautions and preliminaries. I imagine she wanted Yochim to get to the point because as soon as he stepped closer to acknowledge her, she asked, loudly, bluntly—

"Just *where* are they *transplanting* these wolves *from*?" The title of this weekly talk, after all, was advertised, "A Missing Howl."

Yochim backed away, veered toward a lectern to his left with banks of switches and a slide projector remote control with a thin, black cord snaking into a panel. Lights dimmed and the screen above him glistened with an image of a high mountain vista. Taking a moment, apparently, to shake off the woman's tone, it seemed to me just then that Yochim had to remind himself to smile—

"We'll talk about that in a moment. But thanks for asking. That's a *great* prelude."

Among the things I had heard already in Yellowstone that summer was that, geographically speaking, it's considered a high volcanic plateau with an average elevation of 8,000 feet and more than forty mountains of more than 10,000 feet—which, it occurred to me elsewhere, much later, means that each peak reaches somewhere between six and seven times higher above sea level than the Empire State Building in Manhattan. Well-known as the world's first national park, Yellowstone was created by an act of Congress and President Ulysses S. Grant in 1872—some fifty-six years before the National Park Service itself was established in 1916. At the time, history books say, Washington was under pressure from railroad and travel industry lobbyists back East who, frankly, had more interest in Yellowstone as a scenic curiosity for tourists than as a laboratory or nature preserve. The public imagination had been seized by newspaper accounts of geysers, hot springs, boiling mud pots and vents of steaming sulphur sent up straight from hell. Within 200 feet of the surface, ground temperatures were found later to reach more than 300 degrees. The area is now known to harbor more than 10,000 active geothermal features, the densest concentration on the planet. It has more than 3,000 geysers, accounting for 70 percent of the world's existing total. Twenty-five percent (more than a hundred) are found in the Old Faithful area alone. So when map makers drew arbitrary lines through all this open, bizarre, bubbling terrain at the behest of economic and political concerns more than 120 years ago, they ended up with an area larger than the states of Rhode

Island and Connecticut combined, 2.2 million acres of Wyoming, Montana and Idaho backcountry spanning rough distances of sixty-two by fifty-two miles.

In recent years, Yellowstone has also come to be regarded as the core of a much larger *biosphere reserve* known as the Greater Yellowstone Ecosystem—eighteen million acres or 28,000 square miles stretching north to Bozeman, Montana, west to Rexburg, Idaho, east to Cody, Wyoming and south past Grand Teton National Park, Jackson Hole and the Wind River Indian Reservation. Within those unofficial boundaries, though, less than one-fifth of all land remains in private ownership. Most of the region, 13.9 million acres, is controlled by the federal government in a tangle of political jurisdictions and resource bureaucracies: 62 percent falls within seven national forests (*Beaverhead, Bridger-Teton, Caribou, Custer, Gallatin, Shoshone* and *Targhee*) all answering to the Secretary of Agriculture; 14 percent is protected as three national parks (*Yellowstone, Grand Teton* and the *Rockefeller Memorial Parkway*) all answering to the Secretary of the Interior; and 3 percent is controlled by the Bureau of Land Management, the Bureau of Reclamation and two wildlife refuges (the *Red Rock Lakes National Wildlife Refuge* due west of West Yellowstone, Montana and the *National Elk Refuge* on the outskirts of Jackson). The remaining 2 percent of the ecosystem is owned by the three states and the governments of sixteen counties. (All in all, though, I found that you could stumble around the area that summer without knowing who owns what so long as you kept one simple distinction between the forests and parks in mind—the parks usually don't let you shoot the animals or graze your cows.)

Yellowstone today is described commonly as among the world's most beloved and besieged wilderness spaces. A road system originally designed by the U.S. Cavalry now carries more than three million visitors through Yellowstone every year, most compressed into six peak months between May and October when as many as 20,000 people pour through the park's five entrance stations every day.

The average length of each visitor's stay, meanwhile, is estimated to be less than a day and a half. As with all national parks, gate receipts are channeled directly to general funds at the U.S. Treasury, where they may or may not find their way back to help cover the park's annual operating costs and a reported backlog of some $2 billion worth of repairs to its infrastructure. As an administrative entity, all told, Yellowstone sustains something like 5,000 employees and 2,000 buildings, thirteen campgrounds with more than 2,000 individual campsites, thirty-six picnic areas, seven visitor centers, fifteen ranger stations, three fire lookouts, a marina and 370 miles of paved roads. In the backcountry, there are another 300 campsites and 1,200 trails that require occasional maintenance. Even so, through the years Yellowstone has managed to hang onto its wilderness somehow. Less than 2 percent of the park was said to be developed by 1993, and officials said they wanted it to stay that way, fueling speculation that it was fast approaching a future as a natural history theme park, a place that more or less deliberately separates visitors from their surroundings. Every year, I heard time and again, there was more and more talk around Yellowstone of limiting visits, restricting access and sealing the masses inside a monorail train just like Disneyland.

With slide-projector clicker in hand, Yochim began his formal presentation by guiding his audience at Old Faithful through images of geysers, rivers and mountains ranges, building a foundation for a remark that the park was now known to function as the heart of one of the last virtually-intact ecosystems left in the temperate zones of the planet.

"What makes an *ecosystem*?" Yochim asked the audience rhetorically, not grilling anybody in particular and not waiting for anybody to provide a particular answer.

"An *ecosystem* is a place where all the animals and plants still interact together—and we've got that right here in Yellowstone."

Yochim flashed through pictures of animals and recited recent population counts—30,000 elk; 3,000 bison; 1,000 moose; 500 big horn sheep; 500 antelope; 220 grizzly bears. More than 200 species of birds.

"A wildlife paradise, then, an essentially intact ecosystem. But there is *one* animal missing. That animal has been called the greatest test of human wisdom and good intentions. That animal evokes more emotions in people than any other predator."

Slides changed.

"That animal is the animal that exerts the primary evolutionary pressure on these animals, its prey, forcing them to evolve and adapt, to be the fastest and strongest animals they can be."

Another change. A wolf appeared on screen.

"That animal is the wolf. The gray wolf is the animal that used to live in Yellowstone. Latin name: *Canis lupus.* This is the animal I'm going to talk about tonight."

Wolves have roamed the Yellowstone area for at least the last thousand years, Yochim said, especially in the northern range where there are lower elevations, milder winters and, consequently, a greater variety and quantity of prey for them to catch and eat.

Images depicting Yellowstone's northern range were replaced by early photographs of the park and its first official keepers.

Wolves were not hunted aggressively in Yellowstone until fourteen years after the park was founded, Yochim said, when the U.S. Cavalry arrived in 1886 to fight forest fires, curtail poaching by hunters and reduce predation by large carnivores on big game herds. Soldiers apparently shot wolves whenever they had a chance, Yochim said, but the population was not decimated by any measure. Then in 1914, Congress ordered the eradication of wolves from all federal lands, including parks.

"The fledgling National Park Service, believing it was in the best interests of their big game herds, went along with this program."

All told, 139 wolves were killed inside the park in a twelve-year period, Yochim said. About 59 percent were pups. Most were killed with guns and clubs. Yochim said that there indeed have been sporadic sightings of wolves in Yellowstone in all the years since.

"We do believe that there have been *occasional* wolves, singles usually, traveling south out of Canada, just passing through Yellowstone. But basically we do not believe there has been a *breeding* population of wolves here in all that time.

"Things for the wolf began to change in the 1960s," Yochim added, a slide or two later. "It was about that time that Americans began to look at the environment with a different eye. Americans began to realize that *predators* play a pretty important role in nature—that they have an intrinsic right to exist, but also that they have an important role in regulating population numbers in the wild. That attitude change towards predators and animals in general culminated in 1973 with the passage of the Endangered Species Act. That's one of the strongest acts in American environmental history. Renewed overwhelmingly in 1988, it directs the U.S. Fish and Wildlife Service to work for the protection and reestablishment of any endangered species.

"It is this *law*, the 1973 Endangered Species Act, that is the reason we are trying to reintroduce wolves to Yellowstone. It is *required* by law that they be reintroduced to Yellowstone."

For the next several minutes, Yochim's trigger finger on the slide remote seemed to slow down. He tried to explain some two decades of haggling and political impasse, how two wolf recovery plans languished in Washington without action for a total of eleven years (the first was completed in 1980, the second in 1987) and how environmental groups sued the federal government in 1991 for neglecting its obligation to uphold the ESA. Yochim then described Congress's 1982 landmark amendment to the ESA calling for the creation of a new *experimental/nonessential* designation of animals for situations where there was strong local resistance to the reintroduction of an endangered species.

"In this case, wolves *could* be shot or harassed by ranchers who saw those wolves prey on their livestock. Normally, you cannot touch an endangered species."

Yochim flashed more slides of park scenery as he described the current status of the wolf proposal, how the U.S. Fish and Wildlife Service just two weeks earlier had released a Draft Environmental Impact Statement, the first formal step in an approval process that eventually might allow packs of wolves to be trapped in western Canada for release in Yellowstone.

"*That's* what's making this plan so controversial, that we would be actively, *physically* bringing wolves back into this area."

Yochim offered a slide with a map of western states highlighting the proposed wolf recovery areas in Yellowstone and central Idaho. The DEIS called for wolves to remain listed as endangered in the region until ten pairs of wolves had each reproduced successfully in those areas for three consecutive years. The process was expected to take ten to fifteen years, concluding, perhaps, as early as the year 2002 at a total projected expense of $6.7 million. At that point, the DEIS spelled out, the wolf would be *delisted* as an endangered species throughout the region and management of the animal outside the park would be handed over to existing state and tribal wildlife agencies.

"Ten *breeding pairs* of wolves is ten *packs*. Ten packs is about a hundred to a hundred and fifty animals. Ten packs is the minimum number of wolves biologists consider necessary to maintain a healthy, viable, genetically-diverse population in Yellowstone."

Yochim then made an attempt to speak to concerns raised by groups opposed to wolf recovery—namely, people who make a living from ranching, outfitting and resource-extraction industries on land surrounding the park.

"There's a little opposition coming from the logging and the mining industries who are concerned that the presence of wolves will mean that land will be closed off to them. They need not be concerned, though, because the only land that's going to be closed because of wolves is here in Yellowstone National Park. There will be no lands closed because of wolves *outside* the park so the logging and mining industries will be able to continue their activities.

"Big game hunting outside the park is a major source of income every fall. But we expect the effect of wolves on the hunt outside the park will be rather minimal, that the hunts will have to be curtailed by no more than fifteen percent. It should be remembered that hunters do not target young prey like wolves do. Hunters target trophy animals."

Yochim cited projections for how much current prey populations were expected to decrease with wolves inside the park: elk, 5 to 20 percent; mule deer and bison, 20 percent; moose, 15 percent. Big horn sheep numbers were not expected to change much at all, Yochim said, because they tend to escape from wolves in steep, rocky terrain. Wolf packs generally make kills about every two to eight days and each wolf usually eats the equivalent of five to twelve pounds of meat a day.

"Here in the Yellowstone area, we believe that about 85 percent of their diet would be these guys, *elk*, because there are so many of these large animals in the area. The remaining 15 percent of their diet would be bison, mule deer and moose, with an occasional beaver thrown in here and there.

"As would be expected of predators, they will *tend* to prey on the old, the lame, the sick and the young, animals weakened by winter, like this guy, for example. Those animals that remain will probably be healthier overall because there will be reduced competition for food in the wintertime."

Slides changed. More and more critters with antlers. More snow.

"Yellowstone Park is literally *begging* to have wolves. It is *teeming* with prey. Fact is, there is more meat per prospective wolf here in Yellowstone now than there is anywhere else on the continent. That's pretty amazing."

Yochim didn't mince words, though, when it came to cattle ranching. He said wolves would probably kill domestic livestock outside the park on occasion. He cited statistics from Minnesota, however, where wolves take only a fraction of 1 percent of all of available livestock in wolf range.

"The situation would be very different here in the Yellowstone area. The area will have both fewer wolves and fewer ranches compared to Minnesota. Wolves here are not going to be ranging right in and among livestock like in Minnesota. Their main range would be right here in Yellowstone National Park, where there are no cattle and no sheep."

He also cited projections that suggested wolves would take fewer than nineteen cows and sixty-eight sheep around Yellowstone each year.

"What are we going to do about these losses? Well, here's where the *experimental* designation comes in real handy. A rancher who witnesses wolves preying on his livestock can go out and kill them."

Hearing this, a girl in the row ahead of me grabbed her mother's arm and moaned, way out loud—"*Nnooo.*"

Yochim seemed to look in the direction of where the voice had come out of the dark.

"Now, I know that's a pretty *contentious* issue. Environmentalists don't like it because it means a rancher has some control. But the ranchers are not going to let wolves in Yellowstone without that designation. So it's probably for the best."

He mentioned a $100,000 fund raised by Defenders of Wildlife to compensate ranchers for livestock losses to wolves.

"But it should be remembered that loss of a cow or sheep is usually not the only loss to a rancher. There is the time spent investigating the loss. There's loss of fencing. There's a lot of other things that go into maintaining a ranch."

Slides changed then and the audience suddenly was shown a litter of cute, captive wolf pups, a blur of big-eyed fuzzy balls, romping, nuzzling and cuddling about their mother as she lay quietly in a pen. Yochim stopped and looked up, I remember, as a warm, collective sigh rose from the voices of many children throughout the room.

I also remember, to be perfectly honest, that I turned my own eyes away from the screen in that moment. Maybe I was surprised to see such a picture as this, while Yochim was depicting the views of ranchers opposed to wolf reintroduction. Maybe I was still harboring a notion then that it might be dirty pool to resort to persuasions of emotion over intellect if, on the face of things, you were appealing for compromise.

"It's good to put this into perspective," Yochim said. "Logging and mining account for less than ten percent of the economy of this area and ranching is less than twenty percent. Park visitation and tourism, that's over forty percent of the economy of the Greater Yellowstone area.

"We expect that the presence of wolves will draw more people, therefore money, into this area."

Yochim cited a 1985 public opinion survey of park visitors in which six out of seven respondents said the presence of wolves would enhance their visit to Yellowstone. Among the respondents to the 1987 wolf recovery plan, which included all fifty states, Yochim said, 85 percent supported wolf reintroduction.

"So people are pretty much in favor of it.

"That brings up the very last issue—*Will we be safe?* It comes as a surprise for many people that even though the black bear, the grizzly bear, the mountain lion and the domestic dog have all been known to kill people, there is not one *documented* case of a healthy, wild wolf killing a person in all of U.S. history."

Yochim eased the houselights back to their original cast and returned to his spot by the junior ranger in the front row.

"It is the official position of the National Park Service that we would like to see wolves reintroduced to Yellowstone. We do, however, have to submit to the authority of the Environmental Impact Statement. So we will have to wait until it's gone through its full process."

"So that's wolf recovery in Yellowstone," Yochim said, clasping his hands behind him. "It is an emotional issue. Reintroducing wolves, bottom line, comes down to *education*, educating people about what this animal is really like.

"Is it the fairy tale animal that dresses up in a *red cape* and goes after little girls? Or is it the animal that is a powerful *predator*, a very complex and intelligent animal?"

Yochim ended by reciting an excerpt from "Thinking Like A Mountain," Aldo Leopold's essay about wolves in *A Sand County Almanac*, and by playing a short recording of wolf howls. Silence swallowed the room as he switched the tape machine off.

"Hopefully, *someday*," he said, "we'll be able to hear wolf howls like that *outside* instead of inside."

Belgrade, Montana

AS IT WAS, RAY PAUNOVICH ALREADY MAY HAVE DONE MORE than just *hear* wolves in the Yellowstone backcountry. As a professional wildlife cinematographer, he may have been the first visitor in modern Yellowstone to capture one on film.

I met Paunovich in early July at the door of his new house in Belgrade, Montana, in a subdivision outside Bozeman that required complicated, detailed directions to find. Earlier, over the phone, he had joked that he himself had become part of the biggest *real* threat facing the American West these days—*development*.

"I've only lived around here six years, and I've seen incredible changes. Just the *cost* of everything."

People come up from California to buy little *ranchettes*, he said, and then get pissed off when deer start eating after their flowers and shrubs. Paunovich's own new digs were so new, though, I noticed that he didn't have a blade of grass on his front lawn for deer to bother themselves with yet. Just dirt.

The density of human settlement on the fringes of Yellowstone that summer certainly still could be considered sparse by wider American standards. By 1990, there were

some 288,000 people living in the seventeen counties surrounding the park—about 5.2 people per square mile, as
compared to a national average of 70.3. The population
around here had jumped 19 percent in the previous
decade, though, and was expected, by the year 2010, to
grow by at least another 150,000. By the time I visited in
1993, asking prices for raw, remote real estate without ser-
vices already had swelled to as high as $5,000 an acre. So,
apparently, more ranchers than ever were deciding to sub-
divide their old family homesteads into five-, ten-, forty-
acre chunks for a new tide of greenhorns from California
and back East—people who seemed perfectly satisfied with
parcels too small, too harsh and too dry to handle even a
single cow in these parts.

Paunovich led me downstairs to talk in a finished
basement, an office freshly sod with short-pile, wall-to-wall
carpeting. There was a wooden desk and a swivel chair in
which he rocked and balanced precariously with his feet
raised as he talked. He was a big man, broad and tall,
dressed to work at home in a T-shirt, athletic pants and
high-top basketball shoes with the laces left untied.

I noticed a spot on the wall immediately above his desk
where Paunovich had fastened a framed, still photograph of
the creature that had brought him to the nation's attention
the previous summer. It was grainy and smudged and
French Impressionistic in a way. Paunovich explained that
this was a third-generation image, lifted from a videotape he
had recorded with a hand-held 8mm camera off the original
16mm movie footage as it had cranked across the screen of
his editing deck, an expansive, expensive-looking piece of
machinery he pointed out along the wall behind him.

That now-famous tape actually started out as just a
friendly gesture, Paunovich said. Yellowstone and federal
wildlife authorities had asked for about sixty-seconds of
the creature to appease the media once word got out. They
wanted a small bite of the eleven or twelve minutes of
sharper, first-generation material he had already shown
them spooling across that fancy table, frame-by-frame.

Paunovich said that while he felt he had already earned a strong professional rapport with park officials in the fourteen years he had worked on film projects in and about Yellowstone, he was glad after their visit that day that he actually didn't own these images or any of the rights to them. Busch Productions of Whitefish, Montana, had hired him to travel into Yellowstone's Hayden Valley in August 1992 for a film they were making about bears. As a result, he got to refer all future calls about what he brought back to his producers at Busch.

"I didn't have to give interviews. I didn't have to talk to anybody. I didn't *want* to be in it. All I did was *see* something.

"What I do for a living is I go out and observe nature and the environment. I don't manipulate it. I don't presuppose anything. I just merely go out there and spend enough time and see what happens and try to film behavior that I find interesting that hopefully a viewer will also find interesting.

"If you ask me, whatever you *see* is always a lot more interesting than what you *perceive*. Nature is a lot more fascinating than any ideas we may have about what it is."

On this particular job, Paunovich and his crew were working their way through the Hayden on horseback—his outfitter doubled as a sound technician and they sometimes brought a third person along to help hold the horses—when they had the filmmaker's good fortune to happen upon a collection of grizzlies feasting on a couple of bison carcasses.

To this day, nobody knows for sure how two bison had come to die in the very same spot at the very same time. A ranger who showed me the Park Service's copy of the footage later that summer suggested it was the result of a lovers' suicide pact. Still, the total weight of meat left to scavenge, the ranger said, was on the order of 2,500 pounds.

It was a wide open area without trees, so Paunovich and his crew found a slight dip in the terrain to keep the horses out of sight and carried their gear up to a crest to get a look at what was happening. What they saw at first was a sow bear with two cubs and an older male. The male had a big chunk taken out of his hind end. They had heard the sounds of dominance displays from the adults just as they arrived and, apparently, the male had lost. In the coming days, as was to be expected, Paunovich said, the bears developed a pattern of feeding in the early mornings and evenings and during the heat of the day they strolled off to daybeds hidden in the timber, about 500 or 600 yards away.

One Friday morning, though, on August 7, 1992, after the crew followed the sow and her cubs to film her rooting up caches of pocket gophers for about forty-five minutes, Paunovich decided to head back toward the carcasses to see how much the bears had eaten. When they got within 300 yards of the spot, they saw something black run off like a shot.

"We initially thought it was a black bear. When the grizzlies were there, a black bear wouldn't come in. Then we saw that it wasn't a black bear and that it was some sort of *canine*. Initially, I thought it was a dog, that somebody was back there illegally hiking with their dog. And I thought—*Boy*, this is really *stupid*. If they had any idea what was just here an *hour* ago.

"So I started looking around to see if I could see anyone walking. And didn't. Then we realized when we could see the animal a little bit more that it wasn't a *dog*, that it could be a *wolf*. We certainly weren't looking for a wolf or were even aware one existed in the area."

They knew it wasn't a coyote, Paunovich said. It was too big, too dark. Call it coincidence, but he had also just spent a year and a half working with biologists in Canada filming wild wolves there for the public television series *Nova*.

"This all happened *very* quickly. The animal just kept moving farther away and farther away and it's very tall sagebrush in this area so you couldn't see it all the time.

You could just catch glimpses every now and then when it got into a little clear spot.

"We didn't have time to do *anything* as far as like get a picture or any deal. We were sort of disappointed that we didn't do anything about it. But it all happened so fast."

That evening, after the bears dined alone again on fallen bison, the crew made preparations to stay on site all through the next day, Saturday, August 8. They guessed that the creature might return to nibble at all that meat after the bears wandered off to their usual siestas. The way things turned out, though, they didn't have to wait.

"When we got there the next morning there was not only the sow with the two cubs, but this other male and then this, again, canine, and a coyote. They were all there together. They were all within close proximity to each other."

Paunovich said the creature seemed to react immediately to the film crew's presence. It looked nervous and wary and began to move off, but since the bears apparently had grown accustomed to them and didn't seem disturbed, the creature eventually appeared to settle down, too.

"For about forty-five minutes we watched this canine and this coyote and the other bears. After a few minutes the sow with the two cubs left and went back up towards the timber."

Moments later, when the second bear left, the canine left as well.

"It tagged along in fairly close proximity, following the bears back to the timber. Eventually, it moved off into the timber as well and disappeared.

"Wolves are obviously pack animals and this one certainly *acted* as if it was a wild animal. It seemed to really know its way around the other creatures that were there. But it also seemed almost as if it was *lonely* and wanted to be around somebody else."

Paunovich said they managed to get a glimpse of the creature a third and final time a short time later. They had ridden toward a bison herd elsewhere in the valley to record sound effects when they saw the canine and the coyote traveling together about 200 yards off.

"Evidently, they had worked their way through the timber and were moving back through the sagebrush in the general direction of the carcasses. And again, they stopped and sort of looked at us. They weren't real spooked or anything else. But they were certainly paying attention to us.

"That was about it. That was *it*. That was the last time we saw them."

I asked Paunovich how long it took him to start shooting once he realized what they might have. He was using an 1,800mm lens on a 16mm camera. A similar lens on a conventional 35mm still camera would be something like five feet long.

"We started immediately. As soon as we got there I looked up over the ridge and we got the equipment and started filming right away. What was happening was the bears were feeding on the carcass and this canine appeared to go in and get little scraps that the bears had ripped off and dragged in different places. It never actually went up on the carcass itself and tore anything off because the bears were there."

There was one instance when the canine moved closer and the male bear reacted by charging slightly and throwing up a paw. The creature backed away and began looking for morsels on the other side.

"There was never any kind of real *aggressiveness* between anyone. I think the consensus of all the people who viewed the film and looked at it fairly critically agreed that it *appeared* to be a wild-acting wolf. I guess some of the comments were that some of the coloration on it wasn't typical for a wolf because it had a fairly light chest area and its legs were fairly light.

"But there were like fifty characteristics that said, 'Yes, *it's a wolf*,' and then maybe three or four that said, '*Well, I don't know*.' That's as far as anyone would go officially in making a statement without any kind of physical proof of actually handling the animal."

Paunovich said something of a trace of physical evidence was found when he took the authorities back to search for tracks the very next morning. Footprints were discovered in a buffalo wallow, a sort of shallow dust bowl that bison roll through to discourage insects from burrowing in their hides.

"There was *one* track that was fairly recognizable but it was in sand and by the next day a lot of it had sort of blown away."

Still, Paunovich said, there was enough left for one of the officials to make and record rough measurements.

"His comment was that it was certainly *wolf-size*. Like I said, all the indications that they could get said that it certainly was *wolf-size*, *wolf-like*, and all of that."

Based on what they saw after the film itself returned from the processing lab the following week, wildlife officials estimated that the canine, whatever it was, was probably about three or four years old and weighed about 118 pounds.

I asked Paunovich if anyone had come to question the veracity of his film.

"Nobody ever said that to my face."

When I was shown the footage later that summer, the ranger noted that Paunovich had been careful to pan out to frequent wide shots of Hayden landmarks so nobody could claim afterwards that he had staged the scene outside Yellowstone.

"There was talk that somebody had gone out there and dumped this thing off so that somebody would see it and it would stop the reintroduction program. Those comments were certainly made. How seriously they were taken, I really don't know. But I certainly think it crossed a lot of people's minds."

I told Paunovich then that in my short time in Montana I had already heard that ranchers believed that environmentalists had dumped it, that environmentalists believed that ranchers had dumped it, and others still believed park officials themselves had dumped it based on rumors that the government had been secretly trying to reintroduce wolves to Yellowstone out of the backs of station wagons since the 1960s.

"There certainly were those rumors flying around. But I think the evidence was certainly there that this animal wasn't something that had just been released. Whether it was a pure-bred or a hybrid, I couldn't give you the foggiest clue on that. But I doubt that it was a domesticated animal. I don't believe that a domesticated dog or wolf would have acted the way this one did."

A dog or wolf that had been raised around humans probably wouldn't have known how to get along so well with three wild, feeding bears, for instance, and, likewise, probably wouldn't have been so obviously perplexed at the first sight of Paunovich and his film crew.

"What I did learn in doing that film for *Nova* was that wolves are certainly, extremely shy, secretive creatures.

You don't follow them around and find them. You have to wait at an area that they may frequent, be it a carcass or a rendezvous site or a den site, whatever. That's about the only way you're going to see them. They are very, *very* elusive animals."

"Trying to find one individual like that who has a huge area to roam in, that's like looking for a *moving* needle in a haystack."

I asked Paunovich what he thought was going to become of the wolf proposal now that the DEIS had been released and he seemed, at first, to reply only with reluctance, like he wasn't sure I realized what kind of tricky threshold I was asking him to cross.

"I'm certainly not one who follows this a lot. I've kind of been thrown into it because of what I did. But it appears to me that the big problem is if they do an *experimental* reintroduction they can *control* it. If they wait for wolves to show up on their own, the wolves would get full protection under the Endangered Species Act."

As the DEIS spelled things out, all wolves within the proposed recovery areas, whether they were put there or showed up on their own somehow, would be designated part of that larger *experimental/nonessential* population of animals. While they would still be considered endangered officially, *experimental* wolves living in and around Yellowstone would be subject to much more flexible controls and management strategies than the ESA normally allowed.

"It's obviously a game that's getting played here. It's not a *biological* question. It's a *political* thing. It's got nothing to do with what's right or wrong or what we should be doing. It has to do with special interests, be that political or environmental or whatever. Everybody is sort of caught up in this whole little game."

For years, Paunovich said, politicians who actually opposed wolf recovery backed *natural recolonization* because they thought it could never happen. Wolves had been missing from Yellowstone for so long and the distance to the park from breeding populations in Canada seemed so great and fraught with human hazards—towns, interstates and gun-toting cowboys, for instance—that officials had come to greet wolf sightings around here with the same brand of suspicion that's usually reserved for reports of flying saucers.

"But all of a sudden there's starting to be some evidence that maybe they're going to show up on their own and it's like—'*Oh, crap. Now we're in trouble because we didn't think they'd get here and now they're here. We'd better do something now so that we've got some control.*'"

Some conservation groups, Paunovich said as well, had more to gain than lose the longer and more controversially the Yellowstone wolf question played out.

"If you look at a lot of these environmental groups, they're fighting one another. They all want their piece of the pie. It's become a *business* for them. Their mission initially may have been to preserve something or to fight for something. Now it's to keep their lawyers paid and their lobbyists paid and to hire more personnel and print more newsletters. They start out with a sort of glorious objective and the next thing you know they're just a mere *bureaucracy* like everything else."

The same thing, Paunovich said, sometimes happens with what is supposed to be pure science in Yellowstone.

"They've got collars on just about everything that's in there. But what do they actually get out of those things?"

Paunovich said he once worked on a film about the endangered black-footed ferret during which he probably saw more of the critter than the biologists who had been hired to study it. For eighteen months Paunovich watched ferrets, practically twenty hours a day. The researchers were there for only a few hours at night with their spotlights to radio-collar subjects. Then they were gone.

"They would sit in a trailer and they'd hear all these *beeps* and they knew that there was a ferret that was *up* over *here* and it moved from *here* over to *there*. But they had no idea what activity or what it did in between those two points. The thing of it is that all they get is data. They collect data. So they have reams of information. But is the information worth anything? Is it *useful* to have that information?

"I think what that does is it allows you to have a job. If you actually find out something, you might be out of work. So, you know, you always have to collect more *data*. Because that allows you to get more funding and the whole bit.

"It's the same thing with the wolf. If it shows up on its own somebody's going to lose, because they're not going to have anymore work, because their work was involved in figuring out 'Should we bring them back, or should we not?' As long as that stays unresolved, they've got work to do.

"I personally would certainly love to see wolves there and I would love to hear them and to be able to experience that. I think they're fascinating creatures and I think it's fascinating that a place like that still exists. There is nowhere else that I can think of, outside of the *Serengeti* in Africa, that has what Yellowstone has to offer.

"But people don't go to Yellowstone now to see nature and to understand what the environment was like before we started building houses and paving and everything else. People go there as a place to have fun and go swimming and go fishing and do all these man-made activities. To be *entertained.* Rangers are no longer rangers. They're policemen. They've taken on a totally different role.

"It's a Disneyland with grass.

"You get people going through all the time who see *antelope* and think they're *sheep.* You could probably have fifty wolves in that park and if there was no media attention I would guess that ninety-nine percent of the people that come through the park would never even know that they were there. They'd never *see* one. They probably would very rarely *hear* one.

"Rocky Mountain National Park in Canada has about a hundred and sixty wolves, and it's completely surrounded by ranches and farming," Paunovich said, "and nobody up there even thinks about wolves. Their biggest concern is the elk eating their alfalfa. They're more of a problem than the wolf is.

"So it all comes down to perception."

Paunovich seemed next to direct his focus inward by attributing much of the difficulty society has with perceiving its place in nature these days to a predominance of *animal movies* generated by his own profession, films and television broadcasts that fail to portray a wider, longer view of what life is really like beyond the familiar world of cities, suburbs and farms.

"A lot of nature programming does more harm than good. A lot of people get their information about nature from those kinds of programs. But they're *animal* shows, they're not *nature* shows. They just get labeled nature shows and people have a tendency, especially people in urban society, to believe that that's the kind of stuff you don't fudge with. We know all these other movies are all make-believe, that they're fairy tales. But when we see the stuff that Marty Stouffer does or if it's on *Nature*, we assume that's the way it really is. We perceive animals as being *good* and *bad* and they *kill* and there are *victims*. Those kinds of terms are used all the time in those films. It's this *Bambi* thing and it's just absolutely crazy."

Sometimes, Paunovich said, there are more than two sides to a story and that's messy for mass media to handle.

"You're talking about almost insubstantial entities here because you're talking about things that people can't see. The vast majority of the world is so removed from the environment that they have no perception of the connectedness of nature or their role in it.

"It's like the *fires*," Paunovich said, referring to TV news coverage from the summer of 1988, when images of leaping flames, blackened trees and billowing smoke were broadcast all over the planet as 72,000 fires burned more than five million acres of the region, including about 36 percent of Yellowstone itself. In the end, after the last traces were extinguished in mid-September by a quarter-inch of snow and rain, the collective human effort to control the fires that summer was reported to have involved more than 25,000 people—including two marine battalions, a hundred fire engines and crews, seventy-seven helicopters and a dozen fixed-wing aircraft—at a total cost of $120 million, or $3 million a day. Included in the park's losses were 265 animals. Most apparently died of smoke inhalation.

"The media showed up and it became a *disaster* rather than an *ecological event*. We tried to pour millions of dollars on it to put it out and it didn't do us any good and, in the end, a quarter inch of snowfall took care of it.

"More things die each winter than got killed in that damn fire. More animals, more plants, everything. But we've learned to accept winter because it happens every year and we know that it will be okay after winter is gone and there's spring and there's summer.

"You come back to Yellowstone National Park, if you could, four hundred years from now and it's going to look like it did before the fires. There's not going to be any *black* trees or any *scarred* earth. But we don't have that capability and we don't have that perception. We don't think that way because we're humans and we're used to thinking in our own terms.

"We want nature, but we want to make sure we can *control* it."

I asked Paunovich what he thought that might mean for future news coverage of wolf recovery in Yellowstone, if he expected tabloid photographers to bully through the back-country someday, if he expected CNN to broadcast satellite images of the first litters of pups as they emerged from their dens. Paunovich smiled, it seemed to me in a way that said if anybody on earth was going to be able to get those first shots, it very likely would be him.

"Overall, I don't think that the Park Service wants this to be a media circus. I think that most of the people in the park would like it to be a biological thing.

"If and when the first wolves get released in the park, I'm sure there's going to be a major media blitz on the park. But I think it will fade really quickly. I think all that's going to last about a week. It's like everything else, it becomes old news. All they're interested in is their thirty seconds.

"Once it's been on, that's the end of it. They're off to something else."

Cowboy Country

The transformation of the American plains from a pristine range to a commercial pastureland in less than a generation is, without a doubt, one of the greatest business transactions in world history. . . . The notion of the fiercely-independent western cattlemen, the frontier knights who blazed the trail for the westward expansion of civilization, is little more than a myth, nurtured by the cattle barons themselves and perpetuated by a slew of dime-store novels and western movies. . . . For a nation unused to limits or restraints of any kind, the frontier image continues to be the most powerful and evocative of our national symbols, helping us to maintain our belief in unlimited material progress and the future perfectibility of the human race.

—Jeremy Rifkin, *Beyond Beef: The Rise and Fall of the Cattle Culture*, 1992

Bozeman, Montana

THE DAY AFTER I MET RAY PAUNOVICH TURNED OUT TO BE AMONG the first of the more peculiar working days of my summer. I had been hanging around Bozeman a few days—reading, laundering, catching a movie or two, trying to sort out whether I was feeling boredom or bliss here—when I was hit with a sudden work ethic. I hauled myself into a campground phone booth early one morning with a notebook and a fistful of quarters and proceeded to rifle through the white pages, local and regional, it was all the same around here, one slim volume. By noon, I had scheduled appointments at the Wilderness Society, the Greater Yellowstone Coalition and with a big game hunter who advocated turning much of eastern Montana back to the buffalo. One contact led to another, and still others until I realized, too late, that I had booked my coming Thursday into something of a troublesome knot.

I mention this as a mitigating preface for my first, and only, face-to-face encounter with Tom Skeele. His was the fourth of five long conversations I had arranged in offices scattered all over town that day, so it's quite possible that by the time I knocked on his door I might have looked about as happy to see him as he did me. At a glance, it was clear Skeele didn't care one bit to be bothered here. All day, I had noticed that the practice of environmental activism apparently meant living with a phone propped to an ear, networking, researching and muckraking indoors over long-distance. From Skeele, though, most especially, I got a sense that talking to a total stranger in person, in office space he otherwise considered protected and private, threw something of a wrench into his routine.

A common theme quickly emerged from the responses Skeele gave to the queries I lobbed at him between phone calls. *Read the literature.* His answers and positions were already written down. All I had to do was take the time and trouble to find them. I sensed he wasn't in much of a mood to hear just then that I was already on his group's mailing list and that I had been reading back issues of his newsletters for upwards of three months before heading West. So, while Skeele was engaged otherwise on the phone for the larger fraction of my visit, I occupied myself dangerously by pretending to take notes from a stack he shoved in my general direction while, actually, I fell into scribbling an inventory from his surroundings—

One room over a storefront on the main drag. One window facing rooftop and alley. Two metal desks. Two computers. Two file cabinets. Double-burner hot plate. Scorched tea pot. Wolf calendar. Photograph of earth taken from outer space.

Piles of paper: letters, press releases, newsletter back issues, government reports.

Logos: Greenpeace, Amnesty International, Defenders of Wildlife.

Sign: *Our National Forests, Land of Many Abuses.*

Bumper stickers: *Boycott Public Lands Beef* and *Developers Go Build In Hell.*

Cartoon: Drawing of decapitated "Smokey Bear" with chainsaw in his left hand, his severed head in the right, and two captions, *Be Careful With Chain Saws* and *Only* You *Can Prevent Clear Cuts.*

Skeele himself worked in shorts and a T-shirt with a wolf rendering across the chest. He wore his hair short and thin on his head and long and wild off his jaw, almost like the abolitionist John Brown, I decided. Skeele had told me at some point earlier that four other people, more or less, worked here in different capacities, but I was having a hard time believing him. I knew very well by then that this was his place, his agenda. He said he had been working as an activist since 1985, since January 1991 under the auspices of the Predator Project, which, his literature did make plain, specialized in exposing the failed policies and atrocities of what he often called "*that maverick ADC*" as he spoke on the phone. The ADC is a branch of the U.S. Department of Agriculture known as Animal Damage Control which, to hear Skeele tell it, had become little better than a present-day incarnation of the antiquated U.S. Biological Survey, which for decades had done the dirty work of exterminating wild creatures that had the misfortune of being perceived as a nuisance to American farmers, ranchers and development interests under the grail of Manifest Destiny. Other activists I met that summer simply had dubbed the ADC, *All the Dead Critters.* In 1990 alone, the agency reportedly shot, trapped and poisoned more than 91,000 coyotes, 13,000 beavers, 8,000 skunks, 7,000 raccoons, 600 pet dogs, 100 feral housecats, 255 mountain lions, 247 black bears, 170 snapping turtles, ninety-five gray wolves, six wild turkeys and five musk turtles.

When it occurred to me I hadn't heard Skeele's voice on the phone in a while, I looked up and there he was, turned squarely in his chair, waiting, staring right through me. Feeling pressed for time—I fully expected to be dismissed from the premises at any moment—I then made the mistake of trying to paraphrase and confirm Skeele's position on wolf recovery in Yellowstone. I said from what I had read of his work so far I gathered that he opposed scientific reintroduction under the *experimental* provision because it weakened protection for wolves that might recolonize the area on their own.

Skeele didn't so much as nod.

I said it looked to me like he believed the government was planning to use the *experimental* provision simply because it was politically expedient and—

Skeele stopped me.

He said he didn't like that word, *expedient*.

Palatable, he said, was more accurate.

"They're forging forth with the *experimental, non-essential* designation because it's the most politically *palatable* thing to do, given the politics of the region. They want to go headstrong on this approach, regardless of whether it makes any *biological* or *legal* sense. They're not really trying to enforce the fact that wolves *may* be out there and that we need to *protect* them.

"We're actually cutting them short."

The phone rang, so I switched off my microphone and went back to scratching discreet phrases in my notebook until Skeele finished with the caller and turned back toward me.

"The big question really comes down to what happens if these *experimental, non-essential* animals start breeding with animals that are *walking* themselves down? What are you going to call their *offspring*?"

Skeele said it wasn't right for the government to spurn the idea of transplanting wolves only as a means of augmenting—*augmenting* was another of Skeele's preferred words—a population of what should remain fully-protected naturally-recolonizing wolves. A case could be made for striking down the *experimental* designation in the courts, he said, since wolves themselves had provided the government with ample evidence that year that Yellowstone was well within reach of existing breeding populations in the region, wherever it was they turned out to be.

"It's *huge*, the amount of sightings all over the ecosystem. *Acknowledged? Probable?* Not all of them. Very few of them are confirmed. A small percentage are even *likely*. But they're coming *back*.

"If we really wanted to find out if they're out there, we *could* be doing cooperative agreements with environmental groups, with universities. But the *government* doesn't want to touch it. There's all the evidence in the world at this point that these wolves are *not* geographically separate.

"So it'll really come down to a legal battle, I think."

In time, I asked Skeele what had become something of a standard exit question through my interviews that day. I asked whether he thought all the attention paid to the wolf controversy was overshadowing conservation issues that actually may be of greater long-term importance to the region. For once, Skeele said he was glad I asked. He said he was sick and tired of people who focused too closely on the wolf issue by itself.

"It kills me to see people just say, *wolf, wolf, wolf, wolf*. They're not looking at *prey base*. They're not looking at *habitat*. They're not looking at whether there are *travel corridors*. We should be working really hard to protect travel corridors. That's *vital* stuff."

When the phone rang and, afterwards, yet again, I packed my things as Skeele spoke with the callers. I waved my thanks and, as I took steps to move on, I never looked back to see if my leaving made the man smile.

I was just sitting down to a pile of French fries at the McDonald's down the street from Skeele's office earlier that afternoon when Kim Lacey arrived. It would be okay to go ahead and order without her, she had told me over the phone. She didn't plan on eating.

While I had had little idea of what to predict in the way of her appearance, she certainly cut me out of the lunch crowd straight away. I watched her pull open the door and survey all the glazed faces, then walk right up to my table to introduce herself. I suppose locals didn't usually sling around black canvas bags with skinny notebooks, pens and camera straps sticking out of the pockets.

Lacey said she had been interviewed by reporters and college students all the way from the California coast to London, England. Some of the accounts she heard back were pretty good, she said. Some were bad.

"I wouldn't expect good coverage from the *Sierra Club* newsletter."

I couldn't resist—"Do you get many calls from them?"

"*No.*"

My first impression of Lacey turned out to be about half right. At a glance, she struck me as a woman who very well could have been a schoolhouse principal for twenty years. She had tidy blonde hair, pink skin, big eyes, a measured voice and a manner that led me to believe she could smell through most kids' schemes even before they were fully-hatched. She had come instead to be a spokesman on wolf issues for the Montana Stockgrowers Association based in Helena. She had married recently and moved down to the Bozeman area so, after six years with the association, she now served it in something of a consulting arrangement over long-distance. What she said she already missed most about the job, though, was participating in Project Wild, a separate, non-profit outreach program that ocassionally invited her to talk with teachers and kids in classrooms about the culture and values of the American West and how people should look to that old code to get along better with wildlife.

Cowboys were actually among the first environmentalists, Lacey told me.

"We *depend* on the range, so why would we abuse it? True, there are some areas that are not properly managed. I'll be the first one to admit it. Not all ranchers take care of what they should. But those ranchers will soon be out of business.

"If you don't take care of what you make your livelihood on, you're not going to have a livelihood after a while."

Lacey said she considered her affiliation with Project Wild significant work because it helped fight the demise of an important part of our national heritage.

"There's that air or mystique about the cowboy image that's going away. We're losing that because cowboys out here now, guess what they're doing? They're selling their ranches for *subdivisions*. Turning it into a cement park."

Wolves these days, she said, probably faced a greater threat from all their new suburban sympathizers than from ranchers.

"This country is not what it was in the 1920s," she said. "No longer do we have the open spaces. No longer do we have the lack of population. People are moving here to Montana in droves. We've got *cities* now.

"All these summer homes, and yet they want all these laws that affect those of us who *live* and *work* here and take *care* of the state."

When I asked about the DEIS—it had been out on the street for a little more than a week at the time—Lacey said she really hadn't time yet to read through the specific paperwork, what with all that's involved with getting married and moving. The stockgrowers' association, however, had long-since passed resolutions opposing wolf recovery in the region. Lacey said a lot of her members simply didn't believe the wolf's listing as endangered was justified because so many were doing just fine up in Alaska and Canada and other parts of the world. If you're talking about restoring the wolf to its native habitat, well then, Lacey said, some of her members thought wolves ought to be reintroduced to the island of Manhattan, too, but that will never happen.

"You have your older ranchers, in their seventies and eighties, they've *lived* with the wolf. They've *seen* what happens. There's just no way no how you're *ever* going to convince them that the wolf is *ever* any good.

"It's really not the wolf's fault," Lacey said later. "It's just running around. It doesn't even know all these people are really concerned with it that much. It was here and then it was controlled by the government and now it's being brought back in by the government.

"We think that's kind of interesting. Here the government got rid of it and now the government's bringing it back and *ranchers*, somehow, are always caught in the middle."

One thing Lacey did say she noticed in the DEIS already was mention of the *experimental* designation and that, she said, came as something of a relief.

"Our problem with the Endangered Species Act itself is that there's not enough *delisting* and that people aren't part of it, the economics and the people.

"We can't all be about *biology* and science."

Near the end of our visit, I asked Lacey if she was familiar with a man by the name of Troy Mader and a pro-ranching, pro-hunting group called the Abundant Wildlife Society. He was based over in Wyoming, I said, over in Gillette. I was leaving town early the next morning to go hear him speak way off east and north of here in a little town called Jordan.

After waiting out a moment, Lacey seemed to force out something of a diplomatic smile.

"We don't always go along with him," she said.

It was like the bell curve the public opinion pollsters are always talking about, she said. There are always a few extremists on either end and a lot of moderates in the middle. The stockgrowers' association, Lacey said, had always tried to stay a little closer to the middle than Mader. That way they could have a little more say in whatever compromise was likely to be found in that middle ground.

"If the way that it all works out is that nobody likes the plan, then I think it'll probably be a good plan. If one side really loves the plan and the other side really hates it, *uhhhmmmm*—.

"But if nobody likes it, then it's *probably* pretty good.

"We'll see."

Jordan, Montana

JORDAN, MONTANA (POPULATION 485) IS THE KIND OF SMALL
town where asphalt streets still manage to get muddy
when it rains. It's too far removed from the closest interstate two hours to the south for tourists to find by accident, too remote for picture hounds to sidetrack in search
of authentic cowboys to photograph. It seemed to me an
always-deliberate destination, the sole inhabited point of a
treeless plain separating range, sky and, as I found that
second weekend in July, an uncharacteristic amount of
rain passing between. Roadsides that might normally have
been baked dusty and choked with tumbleweed were spotted yellow with sweet clover and cactus blossoms. Water
collected in soupy pools in the gravel outside my room at
Fellman's Modern Air Conditioned Motel. The Garfield
County Courthouse next door, which struck me more as a
dilapidated tract home complete with chalky siding and a
cracked, concrete stoop, had grass going to seed out front.
Around the corner, Jordan had built recently a hall for the
local chapter of the Veterans of Foreign Wars, a glossy tan
rectangle of prefabricated sheet metal with little windows
fixed high in the walls, the finishing touch of purely prag-
matic architecture, I decided, meant to circulate more air

and light than scenery. The sidewalks outside stopped abruptly at the edges of the lot—hanging like bridges that lost their funding in mid-air, going nowhere—and red earth softened by the weather inevitably washed past the concrete ends onto the road where it would eventually harden, dry and blow away bit by bit if it didn't happen to rain here soon again.

It was at this VFW, the most recent edition of *Garfield County's Very Own Local Paper* affirmed, that a meeting would be hosted Saturday by a local group called Citizens for Freedom and a larger assembly based in Bountiful, Utah called the National Federal Lands Conference. More than 200 people from as far off as Wyoming, North and South Dakota, the newspaper said, had registered to attend Saturday's proceedings by press time and each had paid $40 for the privilege. I myself had driven across the state the day before from a campground in Bozeman with designs on meeting one of the scheduled speakers.

Troy Mader, a leader and spokesman for two *pro-ranching* groups known as the Abundant Wildlife Society and the Common Man Institute, both based in Gillette, Wyoming, had agreed to serve as master of ceremonies and to deliver a speech at a noon luncheon on the subject of "God and Country." Mader, I had learned already from his writings, was the brother of a Wyoming state legislator and the son of a well-known rancher, auctioneer and real estate broker. He had gone to college a couple of years and worked five years for the local sheriff's department until 1987, when his father asked him to help out on the ranch and start the Common Man Institute. Their first project together was called "The Death Sentence of AIDS," a resource they intended for libraries, schools and health professionals. It was soon followed by dozens of pamphlets, books, a video and a series of newsletters expressing the group's perspective on topics ranging from government, civil liberties and the Endangered Species Act to hunting and man's duty to provide responsible husbandry over the environment.

As it happened, Mader was mentioned a second time in that week's edition of the *Very Own Local Paper*. A story appearing under the headline "Support for Yellowstone Wolf Booth Grows" described Mader's efforts to raise as much as $10,000 to run an information booth in Yellowstone National Park later that summer so tourists might hear about the benefits of logging, grazing and mining as well as the folly of a proposal to transplant wolves to Yellowstone from Canada. Mader had told the *Local Paper* as much as $2,500 had been collected for the booth so far and more was expected from upcoming steak-fry benefits in Meeteese and Cody.

As for Saturday's meeting, the first article said, local interest in the event could be sorted into three categories:

—first, the widening impact of environmental laws on ranching and other industry;

—second, a reduction in grazing permits on federal lands which, at times, affected adjoining ranches, the local tax base and revenue needed to run county government;

—third, and most specifically, a raid four months earlier by agents of the U.S. Fish and Wildlife Service on a ranch north of nearby Sand Springs, Montana in connection with the rancher's alleged control of predators.

The Garfield County Commissioners had distanced themselves from any planning and sponsorship of Saturday's event, the newspaper explained, because other local groups were concerned it would be too similar to other rallies in the region where the rhetoric had become "heavily ladened [sic] with denigration of public employees, especially at the State and Federal level."

In the first few hours after daybreak that Saturday, the town became congested with a caravan of sedans and pickup trucks, some with still-blazing headlights, all angling for parking spaces throughout town. While there were indeed a good many Stetson hats, fancy-stitch leather boots and embroidered western shirts emerging on the streets, most of the travelers were dressed in a comfortable, suburban fashion—sneakers, T-shirts, jeans, stretch pants and NFL starter jackets. Inside, firm hollers and handshakes were traded over a table of free coffee and doughnuts. As I installed myself beside a table along a back wall, I saw groggy eyes and grunts, nods and tips of the hat. Hugs never broke out, not once all morning, yet grips of fingers and palms were made often about shoulders and forearms.

"How's Dave?" a white-haired, clean-shaven man with bifocals and hearing aids said as he leaned to sit beside an apparent acquaintance on the bench across from mine. A name tag pasted to his shirt pocket said, "Hello, my name is *JOHN.*" An emblem on a blue baseball cap he wore squarely above his eyebrows pictured a wolf's head under the crosshairs of a rifle scope, with a caption that read, *Montana Wolf Management Team.*

"Not too bad," came the reply. "Ain't hardly anything the matter with me except I'm getting too fat."

"Is that right?" John said, looking Dave up and down. Dave was short and strikingly slight. He wore a bright white, starched shirt and a gigantic, round hat with the widest brim in the house that morning. There was a fuming black cigarette holder hanging from his teeth. As they visited, the two men shouted toward each other's ears, largely because of the growing din in the room. Every time it was Dave's turn to laugh, though, his voice would sing out like bagpipes caught under a porch rocker—"Yep. Yep. Ab-so-lutely. *Thhhaaaat's* right."

A third man sat at the table, right beside me, and greeted the two men. His knees straddled the bench cock-eyed, as if he were settling in for a long day in the saddle. He wore a white hat set slightly in favor of the back of his head. He looked at me and my gear, the paper, pen and microphone, nodded, offered a hand and introduced himself as Bill. The first two men joined his gaze—it looked like they all wanted to know—so I told them my name and what I was doing there. They didn't seem surprised. In time, they must have gotten used to me just sitting there listening, I suppose, because the conversation turned to prairie dogs and how the confounded government had banned all the good poisons that would put a stop to their burrowing underground.

"How'd you get rid of 'em?" John asked Bill.

"Just used poisoned gas."

"What kind?"

"Just plain old gasoline," Bill said.

"Is that right?"

"Just soaked them dry horse turds up, four or five of 'em, roll 'em down them holes and cover the holes. It'll kill about ninety percent of 'em just flat."

"How'd you do that now, Bill?" John asked again.

"Just take dry horse manure and soak it up—"

"Oh, *I* see," John said.

"Just pour 'em with gas. Just plain old gasoline works. But it don't get 'em all."

"Well, it'd help get a bunch of 'em anyway. . . . This one fella, he called me the other day, he uses a fertilizer, uh . . . *anhidious*?"

"Anhydrous?" Bill asked.

"Anhydrous, yeah," John said.

"Ammonia," Bill said.

"Anhydrous *ammonia*, that's it. And he said the funny thing is he thought he'd killed 'em all, you know. The old ones never did come up but the young ones did. They probably had been sealed off somehow. Mine, there are just little holes after two or three days. I was wondering if it was the young ones coming out."

"If they can get sealed off someways, yeah, they can survive. The last one, I dosed 'em up three or four times. God damn, three or four days later he come out again."

Bill said he finally found that last critter all shot up, probably by a hunter in the middle of antelope season.

"Blowed him up. Just scattered all over hell," he said. "Didn't have any more trouble with him. But I gassed him half a dozen times. By God, he'd always come out."

"God damn it, I'll have to try them horse turds, then," John said, sounding like a converted soul.

There came just then the rumble and hum of a live microphone being adjusted on a bandstand in the corner, followed by calls for the conference to find seats, to bring their coffee to the benches and get comfortable. *Come along, there's full morning of work ahead before lunch*, was the general, gentle sentiment of the crier.

Troy Mader stood behind a lectern before them, shuffling papers and transparencies for an overhead projector, blinking, cranking up a toothy smile that would have to last all day. He looked young and squeaky for a man with the reputation of an old coot, tight and groomed with a short blond, receding hairline, a dark suit coat, a striped tie and a pressed shirt that seemed just a little pink in dim light. On first impression, he reminded me of preachers or maybe Kiwanis Club presidents back East. Mader spoke lightly for a few moments, trying to establish a rapport with the audience as a trustworthy emcee, mentioning that while he lived a full day's drive away in Wyoming, his mother was raised on a ranch just east of Jordan.

Mader then took a hand count of just what kind of people were in attendance. He called out categories of professions and interests one at a time—*ranchers, recreationists* and *multiple users, elected officials, government employees*, and, finally, *news reporters*. He seemed to take note of individual faces in each portion before proceeding, including mine.

"The purpose of this meeting is to inform you about how you can protect your rights from an ever-encroaching government. That's really what it's all about. We're here to inform you that there are laws written, on the books, that protect your rights." Mader's voice was warming up to the room by now. It rose and became increasingly earnest.

"However, *you* must know what your rights are and what the laws say when you're working with the federal bureaucrats. And *you* have to insist that they abide by 'em."

Moments later and a few degrees of brimstone higher, Mader wandered onto the subject of the responsibilities of citizenship, government and the defense of personal liberties.

"In many cases, they don't realize how fast they're being taken away. And, once they realize it they don't want to become involved because it's gonna take a lot of work, and lots of hard work. And you know what's happening because of that? They are guaranteeing the *slavery* of their offspring. That's what they're doing. Freedom is not free. Never was. A tremendous price has been paid for your freedom. And what we're basically encouraging you to do today is to learn how to fight for your freedom. It's important. It's *everything*."

After waiting out a stir in the audience, Mader began his wind up to introduce a succession of speakers which, as it happened, included more than a couple of people with law degrees.

"It's lawyers that got us into this mess and it's going to take lawyers to help us get out of it. I guarantee you. Because it's going to be in the courts, to some extent, where we begin to win back our rights."

Karen Budd-Falen was among the first. She had once worked in Washington for former Interior Secretary James Watt, but had since come home to a practice in Cheyenne, Wyoming. She reminded the constituency that the U.S. Forest Service was not created to preserve the environment, scenery, wildlife or anything else. It was created, she said, to provide the nation with a continuous supply of timber and to protect water for agricultural use. She reminded them that the Bureau of Land Management (BLM) was created in 1934 by the Taylor Grazing Act, legislation intended to stabilize the livestock industry, to stop bands of sheep from overgrazing areas so the local cattle wouldn't starve out. She cited legal standing that, for them, grazing allotments on federal lands remained a protected right, not just a privilege.

"None of that stuff has changed," she said firmly. A bit later, she added, good and loud—

"Don't let anybody from the big cities tell you you should be ashamed of being a cowboy. . . . You need to understand that you have got a right out there. That you're doing something that you need to be proud of and that you need to be able to pass onto your kids and your grandkids."

James Catron, an attorney representing Catron, Sierra and Torrance counties in New Mexico, came next.

"Our constitution protects your life, liberty and property. Now *Earth First!* doesn't care about your life. We know they do not respect any of your other Constitutionally-protected rights. Do you think *Earth First!* gives a damn about your property rights? Would you like to live under a government by *Earth First!*? Ladies and gentlemen, you would *not* live under a government by *Earth First!*"

Catron always uttered the name of the organization with great hesitation, reluctance, as if it were bile spilling off his tongue.

"We have forgotten the American way so we create and tolerate petty *tyrannies, tyrants* in our bureaucracies."

Later, he said, "Now, I read in your local press that the National Federal Lands Conference is a bunch of evil people because we denigrate public employees. Ladies and gentlemen, some of our very strongest allies are public employees. Some of our very best friends work in the Forest Service and the BLM. They are people who think like *Americans*. Not like *Europeans*. They think like *citizens*. Not like *subjects*. And they support us in what we are doing and they assist us in innumerable and untold ways. Untold by *me*."

He next came to expand a remark he made in passing earlier that he's part Native American.

"I want to point out to you that when those environmental elitists try to fool you, try to wrap themselves in the image of the American Indian, that's a *wolf* in sheep's clothing. They not only are lying to you, they are violating the very concept of the way the American Indian lived. Oh, he lived in harmony with the environment," Catron said, "but you will never see an American Indian environmentalist. Not a cultural Indian. Because he knows that turquoise and silver have to be *mined*. That Navaho rugs are woven from wool, and *woollies* graze. The lumber industry has fed millions of Indian families. They know that the eco-freaks are a *threat* to the traditional ways of life. Hunting, fishing, traditional Indian ways of life, codified in laws and treaties, are *threatened* by this movement."

Meanwhile, during program breaks, between introductions and moderating follow-up question-and-answer periods on stage, Mader himself attended to displays, boxes of printed materials and a portable computer he had set up behind an empty bar opposite the bandstand. He would replenish his piles of offered pamphlets, fact sheets and photocopies, stacks of glossy stock and office paper that bore his byline and title, "T.R. Mader, Research Division, Common Man Institute." Another phrase often followed: "Permission granted to quote from this Report if Full Credit is given to the Author and Source."

The titles of those reports were invariably printed in screaming type—

UNNATURAL WOLF TRANSPLANT IN
YELLOWSTONE NATIONAL PARK
Wolf Reintroduction in the Yellowstone
National Park: A HISTORICAL PERSPECTIVE
PROFILE OF THE WOLF
WOLF ATTACKS ON HUMANS IN NORTH AMERICA
What Everyone Who Enjoys Wildlife
Should Know
Environmentalism vs Conservation: A Look
at Two Roads

Endangered Species Act: FLAWED LAW, Few Species
Saved, Millions Spent, Thousands of Jobs Lost.

There was displayed on the bar a five-page printout of
a computer spreadsheet that predicted, among other
things, that a single breeding pair of wolves could produce
9,648 offspring in a fifteen-year period. There was a "Wolf
Video" offered for $27.50, a "NO WOLVES" bumper sticker
for $1.50 and a handful of free photocopies of articles and
brochures published by other organizations and agencies.
On an inside page of one of the glossy pamphlets Mader
authored was a box of bold type, outlined twice in straight
lines and sharp corners—

> PREDATION MUST BE ADDRESSED FOR WILDLIFE TO
> BE ABUNDANT FOR VIEWING OR HUNTING. THE PREDA-
> TOR IS TO WILDLIFE WHAT WEEDS ARE TO THE
> FARMER AND WHAT THE CRIMINAL IS TO MANKIND.
> THEY MUST BE CONTROLLED IN ORDER TO HAVE
> ABUNDANT WILDLIFE.

Filler copy of this order was especially common in the
stack of back issues of the *Abundant Wildlife* newsletter
Mader displayed.

They appeared as quick wisecracks—*Why did the
environmentalist cross the road? To cause trouble on the
other side.*

They appeared as imperatives—*New Year's Resolu-
tion: I will become involved in the issues which threaten my
livelihood and my country. From now on, the bug-lovin',
posey sniffin' tree huggers will have to fight me and my family. And we're gonna win!*

Sometimes, they appeared as Scripture—*Environmentalists are ones who 'professing themselves to be wise, they
became fools, . . . who exchanged the truth of God for the lie,
and worshiped and served the creature rather than the cre-
ator, who is blessed forever.' Romans 1: 22 & 25.*

There was a cartoon in one of the newsletters with Karl
Marx and Adolf Hitler standing together above a caption,

"The New World Order," and a unified balloon of dialogue, "ENVIRONMENTALISTS UNITE!"

In another edition, there was a cartoon depicting a pair of wolves running straight out the gates of Yellowstone as soon as they had been released from the back of a van labeled "WOLF RECOVERY." One wolf turned to the other in mid-stride and said, "*I know what the wildlife groups say. But fat beef beats diseased game, every time!!*"

Mader's newsletters seemed to be trained at an audience of western outdoorsmen. Idealistic renderings of wild animals were frequent—statuesque deer, elk and bison, leaping fish, foraging beaver and grizzly bears.

The ideas expressed in Mader's text were unambiguous—*There is no such thing as peaceful coexistence between man and wolf.*

Sometimes, they were angry—*So folks, if you want to let the Feds and special interest groups (who, by the way, have no regard for people and their livelihoods), run over you, that's you're prerogative. You can't say that you weren't warned in advance.*

Mader, quite simply, offered a particular take on issues affecting his readers that they would find in no other media.

> Parasite environmentalism is where a government bureaucrat or preservationist group has an agenda and seeks to force it upon the people through governmental programs and regulations. Generally speaking, there is no real benefit to the program yet taxpayers are forced to foot the bill on a worthless program. . . .
>
> Wolf recovery, spotted owls, wild and scenic river designations, the Clean Air Act, etc., are examples of parasite environmentalism—the most common form of environmentalism today. It sucks the life blood out of the free enterprise system and generally is a miserable failure in producing benefit for wildlife or the environment.
>
> Supply side environmentalism is where individuals or groups take upon themselves to spend their own money on programs that help or enhance wildlife habitat. Ducks

Unlimited readily comes to mind. Those duck hunters have contributed millions to habitat improvement with a good measure of success.

"One needs to understand that wildlife management is an art science, not a specific science," Mader continued in another of his privately-published pamphlets—

> A specific science is something that is specific and can be tested, tested and re-tested with the same results every time. Chemistry is an example. A chemist can mix one element with another element and get a certain and definite reaction every time. That is specific.
>
> Wildlife management is an art science in that there are so many variables that two biologists can look at the same studies and come up with different conclusions. Quite often prominent wolf biologists do not agree with each other in their studies about wolves.

On that matter of science, I was curious to note that the word *evolution* didn't seem to appear anywhere in the work Mader displayed in Jordan. What was clear, however, was that Mader was probably America's chief purveyor of information about alleged wolf attacks on humans and their livestock. Gory photographs and graphic details seemed a trademark of his work. His photo captions were often as colorful as the mangled body parts they described. His newsletters and pamphlets were replete with reports of wolf maulings and killings that other researchers have otherwise discounted—incidents ranging from Staten Island to San Diego, involving every socio-economic group and age from little kids to senior citizens—but especially little kids.

> 1975—Small zoo in Worchester, Massachusetts, a two-year-old lad was savagely bitten on the leg when it slipped through an enclosure opening. The boy's mother and 2 men could not pull the boy free. The wolves did not stop ripping the boy's leg apart until a railroad tie was thrown in the midst of the wolves.

1978—A wolf bit a child in Story, Wyoming. The wolf was penned at a local veterinary clinic for observation. During that time, the wolf escaped its pen and killed a young calf. Wyoming law prohibits the keeping of wild animals as pets, so the animal was shipped to Ohio, where it had come from. The owner of the wolf went to Ohio and brought the wolf back to Wheatland, Wyoming. The wolf attacked and killed a child in that area shortly thereafter.

September, 1981—A two-year-old boy was mauled to death by an 80-lb 3 year-old female wolf in Ft. Wayne, Michigan. The boy wandered within the chain length of the wolf.

"You have to remember one thing about negotiating," Mader told the New Mexico Joint Stockgrowers Convention in Albuquerque in December 1991 (the speech was reprinted in *Abundant Wildlife* the following month)—

Both parties have to bring something to the bargaining table. Tell me, what does the environmentalist bring to the table? Nothing—absolutely nothing. What do you bring to the table? Everything—your very way of life. That's not compromise, folks, that's suicide. . . .

Folks, you can't compromise with these folks. They have nothing to lose. Fight smart? Yes. Compromise? No. . . .

Winston Churchill once stated that an 'Appeaser is one who feeds the crocodile—hoping it will eat him last.' I believe Churchill knew what he was talking about. What did Britain gain when she compromised with Hitler? Where would Britain be today if she hadn't taken a stand? When are you going to take a stand?

There came a moment that Saturday in Jordan when I was caught without pen, paper or microphone. I was standing in line for the buffet luncheon, fingering a white styrofoam plate, waiting for my turn at the steamy heaps of roast beef, mashed potatoes and gravy. There was a cowboy ahead of me, and what I remember most clearly about him were his hands—enormous, muscular, heavy hands and the thumb he had laced through one of his belt loops. The knuckles looked like door knobs. I remember standing there and just staring, imagining that man's hands at work around hammer handles, rope, reins, barbed wire and steering wheels. When he turned to look at me, he scanned me up and down, my conspicuous summer beard, my corduroy jacket, my powder-blue cotton shirt and a silly tie knotted around my throat. As we exchanged nods over the paper napkins, he asked me straight out what brought me to the meeting. He said he heard I was probably a spy for a tree-hugger group in Bozeman. I stammered and I said I was a writer from Ohio originally, that I came West for the summer because I was curious about the fight over the wolves. He picked out a plastic knife and fork and said there was a lot of that kind of curiosity going around. Then he said that I was probably too late, that despite everything said at the meeting that morning, the fight was over for now. There was only one thing he knew that could still stop the idiot government with its idiot plans to dump wolves from Canada in open country just a few days from his beef. When the time comes, the cowboy said, these wolves need to get together in Yellowstone and decide—*Eat the tourists first.*

That would do the trick, I remember the cowboy said, watching me. *A few chewed tourists.*

In the collective drowsiness that usually follows a mid-day meal, M.J. "Red" Beckman, also known locally as "Montana's Fighting Redhead," was called to the VFW bandstand. The author of *Walls In Our Minds*—on sale at Mader's display—had received glowing tributes from speakers all morning as one of the first figures in the West to raise a voice against the encroachments of government. Beckman lumbered to the microphone in what appeared to be a state of blushing modesty, saying he hadn't come to Jordan that day to make a speech. Still, he did manage to hold forth for several minutes each about the recent elections, tax protest, the Constitution and the Declaration of Independence.

"You see, tax protest is our political heritage in this country. We all went to government schools and they would have you to believe that a tax protester is some kind of an *Un-American* individual. But I would propose to you that a tax protester is the one hundred percent *genuine* American because he gives his allegiance to his country, not to government. We have too many people in this nation who are giving their allegiance to government. And look at the mess we're in today."

Eventually, Beckman found a way back to his assigned purpose on stage.

"A lot of you fellas, of course, out here have been in the market at one time or another for a bull. And when you go out, you don't just wanna look at the critter. You wanna look at the paperwork behind him. Right? You wanna know what kind of a pedigree he's got. How did his dad perform and that kind of thing.

"Well, I'm going to introduce a fella you've seen quite a bit of today here. And he gave me some stuff here to read. And I'll read it. But I wanna tell you about his pedigree. I met his father back in '76. Dick Mader, Gillette, Wyoming, an auctioneer. Many of you I'm sure know who he is. But Dick had his head screwed on right a long time ago. He understood what was happening in this country. He had that sight, that foresight. He was able to look ahead.

"How many of you here, ten years ago, could see the problems that we're confronted with today? There's not too many of 'em that have that kind of foresight, that can see ten years ahead of time. I guess that's what got me in trouble.

"But, anyway. . . . He's got a son over here that's following in his footsteps, only he's going to go a little farther. This is the paperwork on him."

Beckman brought a sheet of paper before his eyes and read aloud.

"Troy Mader is president of Common Man Institute— well, I think that ought to include all of *us*—that's a private research group. He also serves as head of the research division of Abundant Wildlife Society of North America, an international wildlife organization that has both Canadian and American members. After some college education and trying his hand at some other jobs, Troy became a law enforcement officer where he found his niche, research and investigations. Mader still works in law enforcement on a volunteer basis. Troy has done extensive research on the history of wolves on the North American continent. He is the author of several books on wolf reintroduction, and another entitled, *The Death Sentence of AIDS.*

"I stopped in at Gillette here, oh," Beckman had put the paper away by now and paused briefly to think, "about the third week of May or so and he was out in the corral, branding and castrating calves. So he knows what it is to try to hog-tie a three-hundred pound calf or so."

There were a few smiles and snickers and tittering.

"And so he's not, he's not a guy with a clean shirt on all the time.

"So, Troy," Beckman said turning to look Mader in the face, "you are introduced."

Mader rose and appeared to accept the applause that followed more deeply than any of the pattering he received earlier that day. Maybe it was the presence of a mentor or the mention of his father that made him appear more reflective as he cast his eyes about the crowd. It didn't take long, though, before his customary ardor returned.

"The purpose of my talk is different than anybody else you'll hear speak today because I do not deal with land issues," Mader said early on. "I deal with philosophy. Alexander Solzhenitsyn says to destroy a people you must first sever their roots. And that is what has happened to America. . . . We have abandoned the Judeo-Christian ethic, commonly called Christianity. And we have embraced Pantheism, commonly called the New Age Movement."

Over the next half-hour, often with the assistance of printed quotations projected on the wall behind him from plastic transparencies, Mader tore through territory familiar to me from his writings, accusing the environmental movement of being a front for a modern ethic that advocates the reduction, if not outright destruction, of the human race.

"If you kill a wolf, which is an endangered species, you face a hundred thousand dollar fine and a mandatory prison sentence. What happens if you murder an unborn child?

"Now, I'm not into the abortion issue. I'm talking about values. The wolf is worth more than a human life. And that's because of a philosophical change. You've *got* to understand philosophy."

Mader motored through quotes from early Americans—John Adams, John Quincy Adams, Thomas Jefferson, Noah Webster—about how the nation was founded on the gospel of Jesus Christ and, in those moments, Mader read very, very fast, something like an auctioneer, maybe, I guessed wildly, an auctioneer like his father.

"But you know, we have a religion today. We have a state religion. It's called *Politically Correct*."

Later: "If rights come from man, as the government now says, we've thrown out God and the Bible and now we are the supreme agents. If rights are from man, they're based on the whim of the one in power. And they're changeable. You have your feet firmly planted on quicksand."

Later still: "There is a universal rule you need to understand. The larger a government becomes, the less individual rights there are.

"Woodrow Wilson said it best when he said this—'*The-history-of-liberty-is-the-history-of-limitations-of-governmental-power-not-the-increase-of-it-when-we-resist-therefore-the-concentration-of-power-we-are-resisting-the-powers-of-death-because-the-concentration-of-powers-always-precedes-the-destruction-of-human-liberty.*'"

Mader stopped cold then, astonished, as if he had just heard it himself for the first time, and looked over the hall.

"*Boy*, folks. Take that statement home."

After reciting two more passages, one from Scripture, one from William Penn, Mader finished and received warm, polite applause. Here and there in the audience heads jolted upright from slumber, distracted stares came back to focus and, nearby, one old cowboy leaned into another one's ear and expressed bewilderment, none too quietly.

"This is Saturday, not Sunday. Right?"

Canyon Village

ON A MONDAY MORNING IN JULY, AROUND TEN O'CLOCK, TWO
weeks after I first met him at the cowboy meeting in Jordan, I helped Troy Mader and his daughter Tish set up a
dining tent on an island of grass in a parking lot at the
Canyon Village Visitor Center, deep inside Yellowstone
National Park. I walked right up to them, exchanged handshakes and howdies, and we dove into the task of unload-
ing their station wagon, hauling fold-up tables and chairs,
boxes and cases of papers, posters and a free-standing,
spinning wire display rack meant for paperbacks. I helped
them wrestle sections of aluminum tube and raise the
frame off the ground. We used duct tape and an extra
layer of clear plastic under the tent shell, a mesh of tan
and white stripes, as a last bit of protection in the event of
rain. There were no walls. It was just a shallow, pitched
roof on poles.

This turned out to be the third consecutive morning
Mader had set up his *pro-ranching* information booth in
Yellowstone. He and his daughter had hauled a sixteen-foot
travel trailer to Gardiner, a town just outside the Roosevelt
Arch at park's north entrance, the previous Friday. They
applied for all the appropriate permits and permissions at

the park's administrative offices in Mammoth that same afternoon. The rangers wanted more than a day to review all the material he planned to distribute but Mader pushed them, he said, and was able to set up shop here for the first time the following day.

Mader said it was a forty-mile trip to Canyon Village from their trailer in Gardiner each morning, an hour and fifteen minutes one-way on the park's old two-lane roads, provided there weren't too many tourists stopping, gawking, getting out of their cars to take pictures of grazing elk and bison. Mader and his daughter usually ate lunch on site each day out of a cooler and paper bags. They bought ice cream across the plaza, too, from time to time. Tonight they planned to stay late so Tish could watch one of the campfire talks.

Mader said he didn't mind having to tear the booth down each night and set it up again each morning. It wasn't the park's job to watch his stuff overnight. It was fair, he said. Five minutes farther south, at Artist Point, a *pro-wolf* booth sponsored by Defenders of Wildlife had to go through the same thing.

Mader said he had had volunteers drive through the park in previous weeks to scout dozens of possible locations for the booth. Old Faithful had far more visitors, but the site that rangers had set aside for such activity was stationed off in trees in the middle of nowhere. Here at least, Mader said, they were in the thick of everything. Canyon Village was a commercial strip, something of a truck stop with rows of cars and behemoth recreational vehicles steaming past. In the end, I decided Mader's booth had the character of a holiday coffee patrol at an interstate rest area. Except Mader didn't serve coffee.

Mader said he intended to keep coming back to this spot every day through August, almost six full weeks, so long as his finances and printed materials held out. I told Mader that sounded to me like an incredible feat, like pole sitting or, maybe, a stunt that radio disc jockeys would pull to boost ratings. He smiled and said other volunteers might come eventually to offer relief for a few days or weeks at a time. For now, though, they were just getting started and watching the bottom line.

Mader today wore jeans and a floppy Yellowstone boating hat that covered his eyebrows and the tops of his ears. His daughter, wearing loop spectacles and long, blonde hair down the middle of her back, looked to me like she was on the brink of her teen years, but not quite.

"Let's see. What do I need to do, Tish?"

"I don't know."

Mader dished out instructions and tasks to her all morning, like he wanted to keep the girl busy and involved and, sometimes, like he was talking to her to avoid talking to himself. Time and again, he called her his excellent helper. Time and again, she did what she was told. She minded him.

"Move this over to center it up. Tish, get me a piece of tape. The wind really plays with stuff—

"Let's tape them posters too, Tish. Now, what'd we do with them repair sheets?"

"They're in the green duffle bag," the daughter answered matter-of-factly. "It's underneath the table."

"Put that in my briefcase, Tish. Put all of those in my briefcase—

"Tish, you gotta make sure these are turned over, all in upright positions. See how this one is?

"The donation jar, let's put it up here—

"Take that and put it in the box—

"Where's the hammer?—

"Let's get some handy, dandy rocks here—

"Have you got *Walls in Our Minds* up there already?

"I thought you'd been through all these, Tish, to make sure they were all right side up."

"No," she said and added, again, just matter-of-fact, "I forgot."

They were managing the same variety of material Mader offered the cowboys in Jordan, with the notable addition of a survey response form Mader described as a lazy man's way of signing up for the *no-wolf* alternative outlined in a Draft Environmental Impact Statement that the government had published earlier that month. Mader said he brought some anti-wolf T-shirts to sell here, too, but park officials wouldn't allow him to infringe on a long-standing, exclusive contract with Hamilton Stores, the official park concessionaire.

At the first mention of Hamilton, I asked Mader what he thought of all the wolf souvenirs the company was already offering for sale in park gift shops that summer. Before he could answer I told him I thought Hamilton's marketing strategy could be misleading people, and I offered a case in point. I said I had coffee that same morning with a French tourist in the campsite next to mine and the man was evidently convinced by the trinkets—all the wolf T-shirts, posters, tote bags, cedar boxes, plastic statuettes and ceramic mugs—that the Yellowstone backcountry was already thick with wolves. I told Mader it took quite a bit of effort in both English and what little I could remember of high school French to try to convince this man that wolf recovery in Yellowstone was still a hotly-debated prospect at this point. I told Mader that the Frenchman had smiled knowingly at me and replied that he had heard all about American prankster humor. The Frenchman said he had himself seen wolves by the roadside several times during his visit. He didn't seem the least bit persuaded when I suggested that what he saw were probably coyotes, that wolves were usually much more elusive and two, sometimes three times the size he described. I told Mader that while it had been an interesting conversation, I wasn't sure I had ever gotten through to this Frenchman. The man had said he had personal experience with how arbitrary Americans could be about enforcing the truth of such things as souvenirs and posted signs.

Without waiting for him to say a word edgewise, I went on to tell Mader at length about how I had spent upwards of two hours the night before scribbling descriptions of the massive wolf inventory I saw for sale already in Canyon Village alone. All summer, in shops all over the park, there was usually at least one aisle, one stack of glass shelves and one T-shirt rack pushing wolf paraphernalia. In most cases there was a sign or banner above the displays, too, that said, *Coming Home.* By and large, I told Mader, I had noticed a single premise emerging from Hamilton's offerings—wolves, Yellowstone National Park, 1993—like *this* is the year it finally happened, like all this stuff commemorated the official return of the world's most confounding natural predator to the world's first and most famous national park. But it hadn't happened. It wasn't true. At least not yet.

When I finished, Mader shook his head like he had heard similar complaints all summer, then, surprisingly, at least to me, he let the subject drop. He stepped away and started barking at passersby instead.

"How are you today? All these materials are free on the top two shelves and the stuff that's setting on the tables will be as soon as we get it out—

"Hi folks, how you doin' today?"

"Just fine," came the reply more often than not.

"Hi, folks, how you doing?"

"Good," one woman said, followed by a note of what sounded like utter surprise once she got a good look at one of Mader's color photo blow-ups of a wolf-mangled ram in Alaska.

"Are those *dead sheeps*?"

Mader by then, though, was working on a woman he noticed staring at a complicated diagram labeled—*WHEN A COW IS MORE THAN A COW.*

"Basically what that poster's talking about is there's a lot of byproducts that come from cattle that benefit us."

The woman kept staring, so Mader kept talking.

"A lot of people's idea of a cow is that it's something that grazes on public land and puts methane in the atmosphere and that it really doesn't do a whole lot of good. But there are a lot of benefits."

Somebody standing nearby muttered something about *multiple-use* and Mader seized on it.

"That's right, *multiple-use*. We're here talking about the benefits of logging, grazing and mining if it's done in a reasonable fashion. We're also against transplanting wolves to Yellowstone—"

Mader's voice suddenly was drowned out by a passing RV with a satellite dish strapped to the roof, so he waited it out and the tourists looked around.

"We have a petition against transplanting wolves here if you'd like to sign it," Mader said once the air cleared. "It's like sayin' it's not the wolf we object to so much as it is the baggage he carries under the Endangered Species Act."

Mader held out the petition and a pen.

"Well," a man said, hedging, "maybe on the way back." His companion laughed. They had their arms linked around each other like honeymooners and they strode away together toward a late breakfast at one of the restaurants across the plaza.

"Well, come back again then," Mader called after them. "We got *lots* of brochures."

When the people-traffic subsided a few minutes later, Mader started telling me about a shouting match he had his first day here with a woman who was disturbed by Mader's horrific blow-ups of bloody animals. The woman told Mader she had just finished a college thesis on wolves.

"Now that lady was *mad* at us. She was screamin'— '*Why do you show all these gory pictures?*'"

Mader took to mocking the woman's voice, recreating the moment like she had been a strung-out soprano.

Tish giggled.

"Because, Lady," Mader said in his own voice, "I want you to understand there's impacts. They aren't warm, furry, fuzzy little critters—

"'*Well, you shouldn't show these pictures,*'" Mader's squeaky voice interrupted his own. "'*That's just what they naturally do.*'"

Mader said the woman was furious about his claims that wolves aren't native to Yellowstone itself. He dramatized the rest of the encounter with brash gestures, continuing to play both parts by himself. Tish put a hand over a smile. I wasn't sure if she was old enough yet to be laughing *at* her father as much as *with* him. But she did look around to see if anybody else was watching. They were exposed to the world out in the middle of this parking lot.

"Oh, she jumped in my face about that. I said, Do you know what fossil evidence they have to establish that wolves were here *nine hundred and sixty-seven* years ago?

"She says, 'Well, no.'

"I say, *two toe bones*. Two little toe bones they think are *woolvies*. Now, let me ask you a question. Those bones were carried into a cave by a rat. That's what they tell us. Does that establish a viable pack population because a rat happened to pick up a couple of *toe bones*? What mighta happened is some old wolf was chasing a moose and got his guts kicked out and the old rat picked up and scavenged on 'em. But that doesn't establish a wolf *pack* in here."

After a minute or two of sorting pamphlets, Mader tore into a second story.

"Now, we had an older lady come in who was the typical wolf-lover extraordinaire. Had a big, huge sweatshirt, a big wolf on it and the whole nine yards. The romantist type. And she came up to me and she says, '*I want to talk to you about what problems you have about wolves bein' in Yellowstone Park.*'

"And we set down and talked for an hour. She wanted to see what my problem was. So I set down and talked about the management problems and not havin' the flexibility and all these things. And when we got done that night she said, '*You're the most logical, rational person I have talked to about wolf recovery.*'"

Mader looked at me then like he was waiting for something, so I said it sounded like they had had a couple of memorable days here already.

"Well, yesterday was fun because we had more people on our side or wanting to listen than we had screamers—"

"And our whole—almost our whole—petition is almost already signed up," Tish said, proudly.

"Yeah," Mader said. "We only had like four signatures our first day. Then the rest of 'em came yesterday."

Mader told me he was convinced that the park rangers had been told to keep a close eye on every move he made inside the park. He said one ranger gave him a hard time the day before because he needed to have the booth's disclaimer displayed more prominently. Mader pointed it out to me, a white sign sealed in clear plastic and taped to hang at eye-level from the edge of the tent—

NOTICE TO VISITORS
THIS GROUP IS EXPRESSING FIRST
AMENDMENT RIGHTS. THESE
ACTIVITIES ARE NOT CONNECTED
WITH NOR ENDORSED BY THE
PARK SERVICE.

I asked Mader if he thought the rangers were trying to intimidate him.

"I think they want to make sure that I toe the straight and narrow. Because if I step out of line they want to be there so they can understand it, see what's happening. 'Cause they can revoke my permit if I get out of line."

Mader searched for, found and handed me a postcard he said he got the day before from a pretty young woman wearing a park employee's name tag. Mader said she had interrupted him while he was talking with someone else, that she told him she had a present for him and then left it on the table for him to find later. I had seen the same post-card in gift shop racks throughout the park that summer. The front was a glossy photograph of a lean, lone wolf splashing through wild, shallow water. The message on the backside was unsigned and scrawled in pen—

They were here long before you were. They will be here long after you are gone! It is their land . . . We are borrowing it!

They have more right to be here! And they are certainly more <u>welcome</u>!

Why don't you work on removing. We'd all like to see disappear. The ignorant!

I copied the message down as it appeared, word-for-apparent-missing-word, handed it back and asked Mader if he got a lot of cards and letters like this. He described a file of "nasty-grams," a stack of insults and threats he kept back at his office. He said he sometimes got newspaper clippings about him in the mail with his face scribbled over or targeted under rifle-scope cross hairs.

"I'd say I've had half a dozen to a dozen death threats at different times over about a year period. Real hot for a while."

I asked how seriously he had taken them, and he started hammering the tent stakes farther into the ground.

"Oh, it doesn't bother me. I could care less. See, most of the people that are on the other side don't have the sense that I've got."

He mumbled something about ambushes that I couldn't quite make out.

"I have had some phone calls, well, I can't say they were death threats, but I mean, I took 'em as death threats just by the way they were.

"I had a guy call me up and he wasn't a crazy *wacko*, you know, that's the way they usually sound—you know, all that kind of *rantin'* and *ravin'*.

"But I got a phone call one day, the guy asked for me, so they routed it to me and I said, '*This is Troy.*'

"And he said, '*Hi. Are you the guy that opposes wolf recovery in Yellowstone?*'

"I said, '*Yeah, we oppose it. We see a lot of management problems with it. Not being able to manage them creates some problems—.*'

"Then he said, '*You know, I don't really think you know who you're against and the power that's pushin' this. And you better lay off before it's too late.*'

"Click.

"Just like that. Calm. Cool. Collect. Just about that tone of voice. No hype. No nothin'."

Mader started hammering stakes again.

"I took that one fairly serious. It didn't deter anything I was doin'. But at the same time—*Hi folks,* how you doin?"

Mader noticed he had company standing around. He tossed the hammer aside for Tish to put away.

"All the materials are free, except for the video on the table. These two top rows are free. Help yourself and then the prices are on other things. If you have any questions feel free to ask—."

No questions came from that wave. A few minutes later I asked Mader if he thought he was changing many minds out here. He came back confident.

"Yeah. Some. Yep. Well, some come and ask questions. They're the ones you wanna talk to. There's a certain amount who will come and they've already got their minds already made up. They could care less.

"There's a bunch that come that are on your side, you know. You'll see a Wyoming plate or a Montana plate comin' through and they give us one of *these*—."

Mader made a thumbs-up gesture.

"One of the big things about this booth is it's givin' the local people *hope.* We've got a booth in Yellowstone stating our side. Whether we change any minds or not, that's a real consolation to a lot of people locally. 'Cause nobody, but nobody, has said anything for our side for a long time now.

"I had a guy come up to me, I didn't know him, and he said, '*Boy, I like what you guys are doin'. This looks really great. You don't have to tell me we don't need no wolves in this park.*'

"I said, '*Oh, you live around here?*' My assumption.

"He said, '*No, no. I'm a logger from Mississippi. They're tryin' to put me outta business, too.*'"

Mader chuckled and noticed an older gentleman standing a stone's throw away, gazing at the display, trying to take things in.

"How you doin', sir. Come on up. We're a booth tryin' to let people know there are benefits to logging, grazing and mining, those types of things. We're against wolf recovery."

"You're *against* wolf recovery?" the man said, sounding confused, looking straight at me.

"We're against it," Mader said firmly.

The man smiled and, in a moment, laughed. Mader walked up to him, shook his hand and led him under the tent. Mader had found his first kindred spirit of the day.

"We have a petition over there if you'd like to sign it," Mader said.

"For a minute I thought you was *for* it," the man said, still tossing glances my direction.

"*Nnuuh-unnnnh,*" Mader said.

"I thought, '*Oh, dear. What have I got into here,*'" the man said. "No argument."

"Not on this side," Mader said.

Mader picked up a flier and took the man aside to work on him in the distance. The sound of his voice mixed with those of chirping birds. "*That* was an excellent article. But here's the best part right here. *That* paragraph."

Mader started talking the man through a survey response form and gave him a clean, unwrinkled copy from the middle of a stack.

"You can take that home and get photocopies, pass that around, pass that among your friends," Mader said.

"Oh, okay," the man said.

"If you need any information, help yourself."

A minute or two later, I approached the same man at a rack and tried to talk to him myself. I asked if he was from around here.

He looked me over again and he said—"*Nope.*"

And that was it.

Once, while her father was working on a small bunch of tourists off to the side, I asked Tish what she would have been doing with her summer if she weren't helping out here.

"Probably be at home doin' chores." She didn't offer to explain what kind.

"Well," I said, "at least this way you get to see some of the park."

She said—"Yeah."

And that was it.

So I said "Yeah," too, just to be tidy.

By now I'd been able to figure out that Mader was talking to these tourists about the president, Mrs. Clinton and an oncoming debate in Washington over health care reform.

"—I don't know. I might have to disagree with you a little bit. I got a hunch that maybe she's got it screwed up so bad because he can't make a decision on his own."

Mader laughed like he thought that was a really good one, but the tourists just looked at him, then at each other, and within moments this bunch had slipped away and Mader had moved on to another.

Tish got up from her chair to fiddle with one of the displays and I asked her—"You read all this stuff?"

"Nope. I haven't read hardly any of it," she said, ripping strips of tape off a roll to hold some pages down in the wind.

"That's why he does all the talkin'."

Then, out of the blue, out of nowhere, I asked—"Do you get hassled by your friends 'cause of this?"

Tish turned and looked straight at me, I remember. I couldn't tell if she was annoyed or just thinking it over, but she did look away before answering.

"Nuh-unh. I hardly ever see my friends except during the school year. And at church. But that's about it. I haven't seen one yet up here."

Mader walked under the tent just then, looking proud, looking at me like he was glad I had been able to come see him at the top of his form.

"Yeah. Yeah. Yeah," he said. "This is about how it works."

"What are youse doin' here?" a voice said from behind. Mader turned and saw a young man in hiking boots and shorts standing squarely on both feet, with both hands clasped behind his back.

"Well, we're a booth that tells people about the benefits of logging and grazing and mining, if done reasonably. We're not for over-exploitation and all that stuff. And we're against transplanting wolves in Yellowstone Park—."

The man interrupted and said, "You can hunt goats, sheep and that but you can't hunt wolves." It seemed he had heard Mader's argument before.

"That's right," Mader said. "That's *management.*"

"Why don't you wanna transplant wolves here?" the man asked.

"Won't work. Simply won't work. There's not much benefit to it. And it just simply won't work." Mader went into a lengthy account of the proposed reintroduction process and why his people were opposed to it. "You see, there's just no management flexibility and that's what we'd like to see."

"You wanna *manage* the wolf," the man said.

"Yeah, we gotta have management flexibility. We gotta have management on everything."

"Well, the whole ecosystem is being *managed* now," the man said.

"That's *right*," Mader said. Then he doubled back. "Well, not *really*. Somewhat it is. But here, no. The Park Service for the most part lets it *burn* if it burns. Lets it *grow* if it grows. You know—."

"That's *managing*," the man said.

"That's *not* managing," Mader said.

"Yes, it is."

"That's *hands off.*"

"That's *hands-off* management," the man said, smiling now like he thought he had caught Mader tripping over himself.

"Well," Mader said, "if you wanna call it that, that's fine. But it's not *management* as we see it. Management is when you look at your forage and say, '*Hey, we've got too many animals, we've got to limit the number of animals.'* It's like grazing—."

Mader started to launch into another account about grazing allotments on public lands, the BLM and Forest Service, but the man interrupted and they seemed to start sparring in short-hand, like speed chess, like they knew each other's moves well in advance and this was just for practice, a brief scrimmage to see if the other guy had come up with anything new lately. Appearing to have satisfied their curiosities, the two men shook hands in the end and parted like they were complimenting each other on a match well-played. Mader didn't look beaten down. He looked like he had just had great fun.

"Those are the kind of people I like stoppin' by," he said, watching the man walk off.

A short time later, Tish was sitting in a lawn chair in her winter coat, one hand between her knees to keep it warm, the other pointing to a display easel where a poster was about to be blown over by the wind. It was overcast and it was cold. This was July in Yellowstone.

"You need to fix that poster, Dad."

"I need to fix this poster?"

"Uh-huh."

"What do I gotta do to it?"

A woman's voice interrupted from the distance—"*Tear it up* would be a good idea."

She burst over the open ground quickly. She wore an Albert Einstein T-shirt and she walked, talked and seemed to form opinions swiftly once she was under the tent. The man following behind her actually looked a little like Einstein. He was sucking on a mint-chocolate-chip ice cream cone.

"Oh, that's a *terrible* book," the woman said pointing.

"*Why*?" Mader said.

"Full of *misinformation* and everything else."

"Oh, I disagree with you there—

"I'm sure *you* would."

"—One of the best ones written."

"The whole *booth* is full of misinformation," the woman said.

"Doesn't believe in the *greenhouse* effect," the man with the ice cream cone said, catching up, staring at the aforementioned book's cover, muttering to himself aloud, but loud enough for all around him to hear for some distance.

"What do you think of *grizzly bears?*—" the woman asked, turning and facing Mader head on, "—*They're* predators."

Mader had seated himself by now and he was smiling, leaning back with his hands laced together on his lap. He was twirling his thumbs, one around the other. He seemed to be enjoying this thoroughly.

"No problem if there's management outside the park," he replied.

"Why should they be *managed*? They were here before your stupid *cows*," the woman said.

"Well, because people live here and everything. We have to be part of the equation or we're going to kill ourselves off."

"Well, some of us *should* be killed off," the woman said glaring at Mader. "There's too many of *us* anyway."

"Well, I disagree with that. If you wanna believe that, fine."

"Well. I disagree with your *cows* on my public land, too, but they're *there*."

"Well, there's benefits—"

"You don't pay hardly any grazing fees—"

"There's benefits to it and I agree with you that they're subsidized, but they're not subsidized as much as the tourism is here in this park—"

"*Well*," the woman said. "The park was *built* for tourism. It was *made* for people to see animals. *Not* to have mines and logging and everything else."

"We're not in favor of that," Mader said. "*Not* in the park. No, we're not in favor of that at all."

When the woman seemed fully fed up and ready to storm off a few minutes later, her companion took a swipe at his ice cream and asked, looking at me—

"Where are you guys from?"

"I'm with Abundant Wildlife Society of North America," Mader said before I could open my mouth. "We're based out of Wyom—"

"What's the *Abundant Wildlife Society?*" the man interrupted.

"I'll get you some material," Mader said starting to stand to grab some pamphlets.

"No. I don't want it," the man said. "I just wondered what it was. *Anti*-environmental group?"

"We're a *conservation* group. We're against environmentalism."

"You what?"

"We're *against* environmentalism."

"*That's* all," the man said with palpable disgust, like he had heard all he needed to hear now. Mader tried to hand him some leaflets anyway.

"Wanna take it?"

"I'd just throw it away."

"Well, then don't take it. Leave it for somebody that wants to *listen.*"

It didn't take long for Mader to notice after they had gone that there was a ranger sitting in a Park Service pick-up truck across the plaza, watching the whole thing discreetly through a rear-view mirror.

"Is he the same guy that was here yesterday, Tish? He wasn't here was he?"

"Nope," she said. "That's the third park ranger that's been by here today."

Within minutes, the ranger's boots crossed the pavement and stopped beside one of the tent stakes.

"How are you today?" Mader said, maybe even louder and more hospitable than with everybody else that morning.

"Good," the ranger said. "Glad, glad to see that the opposition is finally gettin' some displays."

"*Well*," Mader said, sounding surprised. "Thank you."

"Yeah."

"Trying to get the word out as much as possible."

"Yeah," the ranger said. "Are these, uh, up for grabs?"

"Yeah, everything's free—" Mader said, launching into his well-worn speech about what was where in the booth. He pointed out the petition and DEIS survey response forms, like he was going for broke, angling, perhaps, to get the ranger to sign one. The ranger stayed by the free materials, though, and picked out two or three.

"Well, I'll just take a couple of 'em," he said. It sounded to me like he was trying like hell to be chipper, and failing.

"You betcha," Mader said.

While Mader turned to consult with Tish about retrieving more material from the car, a radio on the ranger's belt squawked with voices, clicks, codes and static. Without looking, he turned a knob and the noise diminished.

"What's your opinion on the NRA's stand on weapons?" he asked Mader carefully, haltingly.

"I'm not up on what the NRA is saying," Mader said. "I'm really not."

"Well they are, you know, backing any kind of weapon even if it's fully automatic," the ranger said. "I think up to *grenades* at this point."

"Are they?" Mader replied, casually. He was busying himself with sorting brochures Tish brought from the car. I got the sense he was feeling a little baited. "What's their argument? That if you ban one gun you can ban all guns?"

"That's what they're sayin'," the ranger said. "Even the midnight specials and the Uzis and machine guns, that kind of thing, that's uhh, something that they're going to back regardless because it's a gun."

"*Well*," Mader said, like he had resigned himself to making some kind of response, "we support the ownership of weapons. But I mean, I personally don't see any use to own a machine gun. And I mean, I clearly make that distinction on the economic factor of it. I mean pulling that trigger, that thing goes, *brrrriddttt,* and you lose how much?"

"Well, it has no value for hunting at all," the ranger said, not picking up Mader's shot at a jovial tone.

"No."

"I've belonged to the NRA for several years," the ranger said, "and they keep sending out questionnaires about how you feel about certain issues and that's about as far as it gets."

"Uh-huh," Mader said, drifting. "I don't keep up with the NRA. The NRA and I don't get along real good because we couldn't get the NRA to take a stand on predator control, reasonable predator control.

"I'm not a member of the NRA but I certainly support the idea that you can own weapons. So I guess I'm a little afraid to respond about how they think—'*cause I don't know.*"

He let silence hang in the air a beat or two.

"Well, anyway," the ranger said, tipping the brim of his hat, "I'm glad to see you're gettin one up here."

"Well, thank you."

After the ranger had gone, I looked at Mader and asked what he made of all that.

"Well, it may mean several things," Mader said. "But who knows? If I was to go check out Defenders of Wildlife, how do you think I'd approach 'em?"

I needed to take leave of Mader's booth after about three hours in the Canyon Village parking lot. I had made an appointment for another conversation outside the park, a drive of several hours away, and I was running late. I had one last thing, though, that I wanted to try and get Mader to confirm. I stood beside Mader and his tent and I asked if it was true that he once raised a wolf-hybrid as a pet. He had never written about it, so far as I could tell. Yet I'd heard the experience was part of the reason he opposed wolf recovery now.

Mader grinned. He stuffed his hands into his pockets and spoke casually, like he thought it was hardly worth mentioning at all. What I had heard was true, Mader said, but not entirely.

"I raised a half-wolf one time. It was long before I got involved in this. My wife loved malamutes and she wanted a malamute dog and we found somebody that had a malamute dog around and so we got a pup off of it.

"What they didn't tell us was that the female was a malamute and the male was a wolf.

"Loveable sucker. Man, he was so much fun. But the booger wouldn't leave the livestock alone. I mean to tell you. You would yell at him, we called him Tucker, he wouldn't pay you no mind. It didn't matter if it was a chicken or a cat or a cow or a horse, you know.

"And I said, '*This dog has got to go. All he wants to do is eat things.*' Oh, he was terrible.

"And so I sold him. I sold him to some guy that was a construction worker. Lived in a bus he had converted to a kind of a motor home. And he worked all summer there and had that dog with him. Chained him out during the day, the dog would sleep. Then he'd turn him loose when he got home.

"I think he treated him pretty well," Mader said. "He was a neat critter."

Worland, Wyoming

BY THE SUMMER OF 1993, JERRY KYSAR WANTED TO BE A HARD man to find. He had his listing taken out of the phone book right after he and his hunting rifle got into deep trouble outside Yellowstone the previous fall, after cranks started calling and writing the house, cursing him and threatening acts of justice and revenge. Most wanted the government to clean out his bank accounts and throw him in jail. Some wanted him dead. Still others wanted him to run for state legislature.

It actually took Jerry Kysar a long time to decide he didn't want to be the least bit famous. While his wife and kids grew tired of seeing the family name in the papers within weeks of his return home from the woods, Kysar, at first, saw ripe opportunity in the notoriety brought by the national press. That winter he and some friends published and sold posters, T-shirts and coffee mugs by the thousands. He made appearances at social gatherings with his guitar, singing and poking fun at the U.S. Fish and Wildlife Service. When network TV news producers called to set up an interview with him live via satellite back at the scene with a stack of his snapshots of the incident, Kysar told them not to bother to show up without a full pen and a fat checkbook. Even as he faced the possibility of a year in federal prison, a $100,000 fine, confiscation of his hunting gear and loss of all future permits on public lands, Kysar seemed to enjoy cultivating characterizations of him early on as a modern-day cowboy folk hero.

The following spring, though, soon after the government issued a public statement saying it had decided not to press charges and put him on trial, a Jackson Hole newspaper published allegations that Kysar had shot off his mouth to a Bozeman shopkeeper who had showed up at Kysar's front door one day looking to buy a copy of his poster. The newspaper suggested that in the privacy of his own home Kysar had bragged openly to a complete stranger about what *really* happened in the ten days he went moose hunting with four friends in the Bridger-Teton National Forest.

Ever since Kysar had first come down from the mountains that fall, people had asked one unrelenting question of him. It didn't seem to matter if they already believed him to be a fool or an outlaw, they all wanted to look him in the eye and hear him answer one question about what took place September 30, 1992, less than two miles south of the Yellowstone border—

Just what the hell did you think you were shooting at, Jerry?

Everybody wanted to know what was in Kysar's mind in the thirty seconds it took him to slide off his horse, flop onto his belly, line up his rifle sights and lob one amazingly lucky shot straight through the heart of a big black critter he saw running through burned-out trees 218 yards off—

Did it ever occur to you, Jerry, that it could be a wolf, the first wolf to run wild through these parts in seventy years?

Kysar had already gotten grief from a few friends and neighbors after he returned, first for not confirming his target before he pulled the trigger, and second for not following a strict local edict—*shoot, shovel and shut up.* Meaning: if there's ever a problem while you're out hunting, bury the body and forget about it. Instead, Kysar got mad, and Kysar got mouthy. He reported the shooting to authorities and leaked his own name to the press. He floated conspiracy theories that the government had suppressed reports of wolf sightings in the region for decades to protect its fancy plans to reintroduce gray wolves to Yellowstone from Canada. From the start, it seemed, Kysar must have decided he didn't mind if history remembered him as a dumb, trigger-happy redneck so long as it also happened to remember him as an *honest*, dumb, trigger-happy redneck.

That spring's little incident with the shopkeeper, though, seemed to have a big impact on Kysar's thinking. With renewed calls for the government to prosecute him to the full extent of federal law, and with broadening doubts cast over his character, Kysar started refusing interviews and public appearances. By summer, he had turned control of the poster and T-shirt business entirely over to friends. He entertained hope that history and the world actually might leave him alone someday if he finally took heed of the advice of some of his neighbors to shut up for once, forever.

Then, sometime in July, the Worland, Wyoming postmaster delivered a postcard I had addressed blindly to Kysar's name, town and zip code. For reasons he couldn't explain later, even to himself, Kysar held onto the card and mulled it over. A week or two later he received further greetings through an intermediary and he decided to go ahead and leave his new phone number on an answering machine that I had left running all summer way off in New York City. Kysar had never been to New York, nor, so far as he knew, met anybody who lived there. So maybe he was still a bit charmed by the limelight, maybe he still couldn't get over the idea that strangers from faraway places were falling all over themselves just to see him. On the day he took my call from a pay phone at the Sunrise Campground in Bozeman, Kysar asked only a few questions, made his terms clear and, after a long pause, agreed to an audience.

Weeks later, late in the afternoon of an appointed Wednesday in early August, Kysar's wife Grace took a call from my room at the Pawnee Motel right there in Worland. She apologized and said her husband had been summoned back to work unexpectedly, he wouldn't be home for at least a couple of hours. She promised she would have him call the Pawnee as soon as he washed up and finished supper with the kids. Go ahead and unpack, she said, relax, settle in.

Settling in wasn't as much of a problem as settling sudden doubts. Kysar had earned a reputation for reconsidering interviews on a hunch, standing up and stranding writers and TV people out in the middle of nowhere. It didn't seem to be a matter of spite as much as survival instinct. Kysar knew by then he didn't owe anybody a piece of his hide and, since the incident with the shopkeeper, he wasn't about to invite trouble into his own home if he sensed it ahead of time. So there was nothing left for me to do at the Pawnee that afternoon but wait and see what Kysar's intuition moved him to do, and nothing but a thick file to thumb through with some of the clippings, quotes and artifacts Kysar's life had generated the previous year.

There was a first article published by *The Billings Gazette* on October 7, a day after Kysar dialed up Mike Milstein at the newspaper's Cody bureau and fingered himself as the Yellowstone wolf shooter. The government had issued press releases about the incident in the previous week but had kept Kysar's name secret somehow. Two things, Kysar would say later, motivated him to make that call. First, he was sure the government was trying to sweep the incident under a bureaucratic rug and, second, he had a sneaky feeling the press was bound to find him anyway. He wanted to go public on his own terms with a reporter whose work he had followed, respected and trusted. Milstein's editors in Billings put the story at the top of the front page the very next morning under a headline that read—'*Like Shooting a Dinosaur.*'

> WORLAND, Wyo.—When he and his hunting partner topped a rise south of Yellowstone National Park last week in search of moose, they heard coyotes howling and yapping. Jerry Kysar was determined to shoot one.
>
> "It all took place in less than 30 seconds," the Worland, Wyo., man said in an interview Tuesday with the *Gazette*. "I jumped off the saddle, grabbed the gun out of the scabbard, chambered a round and shot."
>
> At about 150 to 170 yards, using a rifle stand, he aimed at the lead animal, the biggest one of the four or five, and fired as it ran through a gap in the timber. After the creature fell, Kysar and his partner, Lynn Robirds of Powell, Wyo., looked it over.
>
> It wasn't a coyote, which are open to hunting in Wyoming and which Kysar said he often shoots for sport.
>
> It may have been a wolf.
>
> If so, it would be the first one of the endangered species reported killed in the Yellowstone region since 1923. And the first physical evidence that wolves are now back in the area, biologists say.
>
> Federal authorities are still investigating the death of the animal. Wyoming Game and Fish Department Assistant Chief Warden John Talbott doubted that Kysar would face any charges since wolves have been thought to be absent from the region for decades.
>
> "It was like shooting a dinosaur," agreed Kysar, 34, a Wyoming native who has hunted all his life.
>
> Experts said the animal weighed 92 pounds. It had eyes that were "the kind of piercing yellow you read about in books," Kysar said, and large pads on its feet. "The darn thing was beautiful, full and sleek, like a show dog. Looking back on it, it was neat to see it running through the timber." However, Kysar believes the animal could be a cross between a wolf and a coyote or a dog, since it had short legs and was so well-fed, he said. He fears environmental extremists may be raising such hybrids and secretly releasing them in Yellowstone.

If wolves are residing in Yellowstone, Kysar said, someone should have seen them before him.

Biologists who examined the animal said they saw no signs it was a hybrid. Genetic testing may settle that and indicate whether the creature is descended from wolves in northern Montana.

The animal was colored gray-black, which Kysar had first attributed to ashes left by forest fires. Before last week, he had seen wolves only in the zoo and on television.

Knowing that killing an endangered species is illegal, some in Kysar's five-man hunting party offhandedly suggested burying the animal and keeping quiet. But the Worland man told them that was not an option.

And party leader Rick Harrison of Powell, who Kysar said is a very conscientious hunter, agreed.

"I said, 'Guys, we can't do that, because people need to know what's going on up here,'" Kysar recalled Tuesday. So he covered the animal with brush to guard it from predators and tacked a note to a nearby Yellowstone Park ranger cabin.

He asked to talk to a biologist from the Wyoming Game and Fish Department, which, he said, he trusts more than the federal government. But instead, park rangers investigated the shooting at the request of the U.S. Fish and Wildlife Service, which oversees endangered species.

Talbott said that was "a matter of logistics," since no state officers were in the area. And Kysar praised the rangers for acting professionally and not heavy-handed.

The Worland man—in the dark about the federal probe of his actions—hopes if he is prosecuted, some sportsmen's or livestock organization may give him legal support. He also wants back his photographs of the animal, which were confiscated by the government.

"I don't want the federal people using it for their own ends," he said.

Although not dead-set against allowing native wolves to return to Yellowstone, Kysar worries that unless regulated, they may follow big game out of the park, forcing land closures, as grizzly bears have done.

"I believe things should be the way God intended them to be," he said. "But I don't believe in playing God."

Had he any inkling the animal was a wolf, Kysar said, he would never have fired at it. But he hopes some good may result, if biologists can tell where it came from and why it was there.

"All we are is common Wyoming people who shot a damn wolf we didn't know existed," said Kysar, a father of four and employee of Marathon Pipe Line Co. "It never seemed like a possibility."

I found my notes and transcripts in the file, too, from a mail-order videotape recorded less than a month later of Kysar's appearance on *Main Street Wyoming*, a public affairs TV show broadcast by Wyoming Public Television from the studios of KCTV at Central Wyoming College in Riverton. Kysar had been introduced to viewers in equal standing with four other guests on the set—state and federal wildlife officials, a livestock industry spokesman and the leader of a wolf advocacy group based in Moose, Wyoming.

The moderator, Geoff O'Gara, sat apart from the panel and read a windy introduction to frame the discussion before he turned to Kysar and asked that interminable first question—

"Did you know at the time that you were shooting a wolf?"

"No. No. No," Kysar mumbled, blinking slowly and squirming a bit like a prison convict dressed up in street clothes for a court hearing. He took pains to explain that he thought he was firing on the largest and darkest in a pack of four or five coyotes he saw running through trees.

When Kysar pronounced the word coyote it was always the old cowboy way, *KI-yot*, as two syllables of contempt.

O'Gara seemed unconvinced and he pressed.

"This was a fairly *big* coyote if that's, *in fact*, what you thought you were seeing at the time."

"Yeah," Kysar said, nodding, "he was bigger than the others."

Kysar's dead wolf, it turned out, weighed ninety-three pounds, at least twice the size of coyotes indigenous to the region. (Wildlife officials were confident it was not the same creature Ray Paunovich had filmed in Yellowstone's Hayden Valley almost six weeks earlier. Kysar's wolf was smaller and colored differently.) Kysar himself looked to be no more than 150 pounds drawn out over five-feet, eight-inches, tops. Kysar had always maintained that all the other animals running behind his big black moving target were coyotes. Definitely coyotes. No doubt in his mind.

"Good hunters don't go out shooting at a rustling of brushes," Kysar said over the airwaves. "I wasn't out there shooting at a rustling of brushes. I was shooting at what I conceived to be coyotes. I shoot coyotes all the time and I don't apologize for it. I shoot gophers. I kill rattlesnakes. The way I look at it, it was an accidental thing. But I'm accountable for my reactions."

Kysar seemed to gain confidence and composure the longer the lights and lenses were trained on him. At the opening of the second half-hour O'Gara asked Kysar if a fear of wolves ever entered his mind as he had one in his sights. Kysar seemed amused by the question. Maybe he smelled a trap buried in O'Gara's phrasing.

"The first thing that came to my mind wasn't, *'Oh no, you criminal, you shot a wolf.'* It was more like, *'Hey, here's some evidence. Hey, there's wolves up here.'"*

Kysar seemed to be a quick study in the art of TV persuasion. Within five minutes he had taken the image offensive. He asked complicated, direct questions of the other panelists. He interrupted their responses and fended off any attempt to step on his own. He was animated in his armchair. With every close-up and wide-shot of the group Kysar was perched in a new body position. He seemed active, sincere and natural on a stage populated with stiffs. Right there on camera, in front of O'Gara, in front of the entire state, Kysar looked like an ordinary guy discovering an itch to try extraordinary things.

"We've been told for years by a lot of biologists that there are no wolf packs up in that area or within Wyoming. They said that they were eradicated in the early 30s.

"I'm not here representing *pro-wolves*, *no-wolves* or the science community," he said in a sideways reference to the four people beside him.

"I've grown up in the third generation of people that have *worked* in this state, the kind of guy that puts his boots on every morning, kisses his kids goodbye, hugs 'em and walks outside wondering, '*Is today or tomorrow going to be the last day of my job because of a spotted owl or a wolf?*' You're talking about economic millions of dollars.

"I work for a pipeline company and we use a lot of public land. Out here, out West, where forty percent of the land is public land, our livelihood depends on it. And you can't shut the whole state down."

Kysar was on a roll that had only just started at the Riverton TV studios. While he had already proven he was armed and willing, he was turning out to be far more dangerous than anyone, maybe even he, ever expected.

In clippings I collected from the following months, it was apparent that federal officials close to the reintroduction proposal had tried to downplay Kysar's dead wolf as an isolated incident, a novelty of wildlife biology, a scientific curiosity. Time and again in the press a skeptical spin was crafted—*Single wolves do not a breeding population make.* Talk focused not so much on the one wolf Kysar brought down but on the minimum number of transplanted animals it would take to insure a viable future for wolves in the region.

At the same time, it didn't seem to take much more than the mere appearance of weighty deliberation for state and federal prosecutors to decide not to file charges against Kysar. A criminal trial would only inflame the region, bog down the reintroduction proposal and send an unfriendly message to locals about what happens to a man who volunteered any kind of information to the government. A conviction wouldn't have come easy, either. Few juries would expect Kysar, a blue-collar worker with a two-year associate's degree, to determine conclusively in thirty seconds at a distance of 200 yards what it took government experts six months to establish using state-of-the-art genetic tests and exhaustive physical studies of a body Kysar had given them in hand. To this day, government findings about Kysar's wolf are couched in uncertainty. Specific, scientific descriptions of the animal trickled out of the labs and, eventually, into my file only in bits and pieces—

> Charcoal gray; big feet; excellent condition; no physical evidence it had been held recently in captivity; analysis of the stomach contents indicated the animal had fed on an elk prior to its death; estimated between 2-1/2 and 3-1/2 years old; sustained a severe head injury at an early age; some evidence of skull abnormalities; third lower molar tooth appeared never to have erupted; no genetic evidence the animal was a hybrid of wolf, coyote or red wolf; based on the shape of the tympanic bullae in the inner ear and measurements of the upper toothrow, the upper carnassial tooth and overall skull size, though, it may be reasonable to suppose the specimen represented some degre.8e of dog-wolf hybridization; unable to estimate percentage of dog ancestry; otherwise appeared to be a normal wild *Canis lupus*.

Scientists eventually told the public that Kysar's dead canine shared maternal genetic ancestry with a wolf pack that colonized the Ninemile Valley northwest of Missoula in 1987—some 250 miles from Yellowstone—yet nobody knew precisely where it came from or where it was headed. Nobody knew if it was just passing through or if it was scouting out a home range. Nobody knew if, as Kysar had come to suspect that year, this animal descended from a purported rare subspecies of wolves that had survived outside human notice in the Yellowstone region for more than a half-century. Few people had seriously entertained the notion of a remnant native population at all until Kysar threw that round through the trees and dropped this mystery critter on a dead run.

While Kysar himself may never have thought of it as such, his impulse to squeeze the trigger that day broke a twenty-year stalemate in national wolf politics. Suddenly, with a corpse on the bargaining table from just outside the park, everybody with a stake in the debate for or against the scientific reintroduction of wolves to Yellowstone wanted to sit down and hammer out a firm, final compromise. The wolf you know and can control, their experience with Kysar had convinced them, was far better than a wolf that showed up all on its own.

There was one last item in the file spread open on my bed at the Pawnee that afternoon: a much-reduced photocopy of Kysar's notorious poster, the one he published to turn a quick buck and settle a score with the extremists who had harassed his home and family. *WYOMING* was plastered across the top of the design in white block letters reminiscent of old wanted posters. In the center was a sparkling, black-and-white photograph of Kysar standing below a backdrop of lodgepole pine up in the Bighorn Mountains somewhere, posing in the snow beside a horse with a pile of freshly-killed coyote pelts draped over its back. In his left arm Kysar held a borrowed wolf hide as high as his shoulder. With his right he held that very same trouble-making rifle, the stock braced on his thigh, the barrel pointed to the sky. Below, there was a caption in simple white type—

> *Remember—*
> *There ain't no wolves in Wyoming,*
> *Clinton won't raise your taxes,*
> *And Elvis lives in Jackson Hole.*
> *—Jerry Kysar*

They were all lies, of course. Nobody can afford to *live* in Jackson Hole.

Less than fifteen minutes after Kysar called the Pawnee with an address and directions to his house that evening, there was a diesel pick-up with Ohio license plates staggering up his street. At that moment, Kysar was standing out front with his boy practicing with a fly rod across the short lawns of the neighborhood. A blur of fluorescent orange line whipped through the air in wide, high arcs until Kysar reeled in and handed the rod over to his young son. The house itself was a one-story postwar quick-build with a shallow roof and a black security gate anchored to the front door. Kysar walked inside to the living room, kicked off his shoes and planted himself in an easy chair within clear hearing distance of the kitchen door, a spot where his wife Grace would come occasionally to stand and listen to the conversation. Grace seemed to take it as her responsibility to check on her husband, to mind his tone and train of thought. She fully entered the room only once in three hours, though, to retrieve a daughter who had nested and fallen asleep on her father's lap as he was talking. Kysar actually did look like he was just cleaned up and comfortable after making a messy day of it on the pipeline. He wore heavy white athletic socks, jeans and a white short-sleeve sports shirt. There was a scratchy-looking, full day's growth of blond beard on his face.

It was at this moment, as I took a seat on the edge of the couch, fired up my recorder and flipped to an open page in my notebook, that I took the single biggest gamble of the summer. For weeks, I had been thinking about the first question I would put to Kysar. I had rehearsed the moment in my mind so many times that when the chance came it seemed to happen all on its own, I was sitting there and then I heard the sound of my own voice telling Kysar that I didn't think it really mattered anymore if he thought he was shooting at a wolf or a coyote that day outside Yellowstone.

"I guess what I'm most curious about is what happened *after* you brought it down."

"Oh, *really?*" Kysar said. He both looked and sounded incredulous.

"Yeah, what happened afterwards? What did it do to your life?"

Apparently, nobody had ever asked him before, which was, frankly, the whole point behind the gamble. Kysar put aside his stack of snapshots. He looked me over. He sat back in his chair and, after staring through a beat of silence, maybe two, he started, the tone of his voice falling into something quick and quiet, as if he couldn't help but speak below whispers in church.

> I'll be honest with you. It's been one heck of a ride. If I had it to do over again, first of all, I probably would never have shot it. Second of all, I wouldn't have turned it in. It's just so dag-gone political. It's such a hot potato.

> —

> I'd honestly never even seen a wolf before and I'm not a great hunter. I'm not a great white hunter. You don't see animals hanging off my walls. I don't have any heads or anything like that. I like getting out in the woods. I like fishin'. I like huntin'. But I'm a meat hunter.

> —

> I think there was some divine intervention in this whole thing. I really do. . . . I should never have even got the shot off on it.

> —

> It's just like if you're huntin' birds. . . . There's always that little rabbit that jumps up, whether you're huntin' birds or deer or whatever, and a little rabbit takes off or a magpie takes off flying and you want to throw that shot just to see, I mean, not to kill it, but just to see, 'Can I hit it?'

> —

> I'll tell you, I got a bunch of friends that give me all kinds of hell about shootin' something I didn't know what it

was. *Because that's the first law of any hunter, identify your target, know what the hell you're shootin' at. I don't want my kids growin' up thinkin' I shoot at anything that moves, cause I don't.*

———

You'd a hadda been there. I'll tell you what, I coulda let it go, I coulda let it run away. But I'd never known. I'd been asking myself, I'd been kickin' myself today saying, 'What was it?' The chances were, I don't know if I'd a hit it anyway, but I had to take the shot.

———

When I finally shot him he was right at what they paced it off as two hundred and eighteen yards. It hit him in the heart.

———

Lynn, the guy that was with me, he couldn't believe it. That was the talk of the whole rest of the trip. All he said was, 'I can't believe you got that off.' . . . Through the heart, running through trees. It's divine intervention. . . . I think it was due. I think eventually somebody was going to get one. And somebody was goin' to have to turn it in.

———

I left him. We left him totally, one hundred percent there. Because if he was definitely a wolf and he was an endangered species we wasn't goin' to drag him nowhere, you know? I was in trouble enough and I wanted all the evidence there and I wanted them to be able to find the tracks. I wanted them to be able to find the blood. So we covered him up with a bunch of sticks because crows were flying around there, scavengers. And the sun.

———

Sure enough, about a day later, they showed up. And it was a good thing because he was bloated. He was bloated and he was gettin' deformed and they came in and they packed him out and they interrogated us and they were, they were fairly decent. They really were. They were fairly efficient. They got a little obnoxious.

———

The little guys, the guys on the bottom, they played fair with me. . . . They really shot square with me. But the people at the top, I think, are still politically motivated. But they didn't want to come out and hang me because they woulda had this whole region up in arms.

—

I honestly don't believe I'm the first guy in sixty years to shoot a wolf. The people that I've talked to don't believe it. There's a guy up in Lovell and he swears up and down that he's got a friend that shot one down in the Graybull River country. But he said he wouldn't dare turn it in. He said he left it. The way the law is set up people are afraid.

—

You know, I talked to James Watt. He was going to help me out. Former Secretary of the Interior, he's a Wyoming guy. When I grew up in college he was bad news. I mean, we always bad mouthed James Watt. But after this thing happened I gave old James Watt a call and, as far as I'm concerned, he's a saint. I don't care what anybody says, I love the man. I think he's the greatest. Because he stood up for me. He offered. He said, 'Jerry, if they decide to prosecute you I'll raise some money up for your defense.' *He says,* 'And I'll stand behind you.' *And I appreciated that, you know, for a guy that didn't know me from Adam.*

—

The posters were meant to be a joke. Everybody around here was laughin' about it because by the time the Fish and Wildlife Service finally came out and said, 'Okay, we're callin' it a wolf,' *it was six months down the road.*

—

When the Fish and Wildlife Service finally came out and said, 'Yes, it's a wolf,' *by golly, I stuck my chest out and I said,* 'I told you so, you dumb S.O.B.'s. Look at me, by golly. Honest me. I turned it in. Look at me. I'm a saint. . . . I'll be famous. Put a book out. Shucks, me and old Ollie North will be goin' out and playin' golf.'

—

I went through this phase where I was sayin', 'Yeah, my God, I'm goin' to sock it to 'em and I'm goin' to promote myself on this deal and sell trinklets.' And I did. And my wife, she had problems with me on that. And I finally had to come back down to earth.

———

I took a step back and I said to myself, 'Hey, there's people that hate your guts. There's people that think you did a bad deal. You ain't no hero.'

———

I mean, my kids gotta go to school here and they're goin' to hear this when I'm an old man. . . . I want my kids to know that, hey, I'm not a saint. There was a time when this all happened and I tried to promote myself. But it's gone and it's over.

———

Everybody involved in this whole thing is basically good people. They are. They let the emotionalism get involved in it. For a neighbor to hate a neighbor because one likes wolves and one doesn't it doesn't make sense.

———

The sad thing about it is I got friends on both sides of it, good friends. It's emotional. I mean, it's like the abortion issue out here. I'm against wasting taxes. But at the same time, I think it'd be neat to go up there and sit at a camp-ground and hear a wolf howl. I mean, there's nothin' wrong with that. And I'd love to hear it. But at the same time, I work for a pipeline company and if they run the wolf program like they have the grizzly bear program, it's going to be a big fiasco.

———

The thing is, and this is what gets me, is the taxpayers are the losers in the whole deal because they're goin' to fund a government deal based off of government statistics, gov-ernment facts, government findings, everything government and the government is totally lyin' to them. In their own way, they're lyin'. And these people are not goin' to be held accountable. They're not. Those guys are just on their own little agenda and the public—it so amazes me how you can sway the public opinion. It just blows me away. You'll find it more out here maybe than back East. I've never been back East other than maybe to Iowa. But people out here, honestly, the majority of them, they don't trust the government as far as you can throw 'em.

—

Yeah, it's beginnin' to feel a little like hunting season again. But I'm not hunting that area again this year.

You know what would happen to me if I went back in that country again this year and I had to shoot a grizzly bear to protect my wife? They would hang me from the highest tree. No matter if I had bite marks on my butt, they would take me to the fifth degree.

The next time I spoke with Jerry Kysar came much, much later. Once I started going through my notes and transcripts back East, I called him up in Worland on occasion for confirmation, amplification and clarification of any details and little problems I could find along the way. For some reason, of all the people I talked with out West that summer, I think Kysar was the one person I tried hardest to hear, whatever it was he wanted to say, whenever, however he wanted to say it.

It always seemed important to him, for instance, that I understand he never meant to get stinking rich off of his role in what happened. Even with the posters, he said he had cleared just enough with his end to buy a barbecue, a couple of rifles and, maybe, enough to take Grace out to dinner a few times. He always took pains to remind me that, at first, he and a friend had them printed up just as little postcards, as a joke to be shared with immediate family and friends. Then, after the first 200 copies they had made into full-blown posters sold out at a local bar in a single weekend, they decided to print more. Then more, and more again, so many times that Kysar quickly lost count. They were still selling even now, Kysar said, even after all this time. But, no, he wasn't getting rich. Hell, all together, he'd probably *given* a thousand of the things away.

"If I was out to make money on this, I woulda charged ten, fifteen bucks on them posters. There were people that bought 'em off me for five dollars that turned around and charged twenty-nine bucks."

It also always seemed important to Kysar that I understand that he never, not for one moment, was ever proud of what he had done.

"I didn't do it out of maliciousness. I didn't try and hide it. As soon as I seen what it was, I thought, *'Man, this is a scientific* find. *Let's get some people that need to know about what's going on here.'*

"It's one thing to know they're there and shoot 'em. But, honest, I'm not a poacher. If I'd a known there were wolves in the area, I'd a never shot it.

"I can't believe this thing went as far as it did. Shucks, I'd barely even had a traffic ticket before.

"Honestly, before all this happened, I didn't know diddle about wolves. But now I think I should get an honorary four-year degree from the University of Montana in wolf studies. I think I understand 'em pretty good."

Eventually, Kysar would always get around to talking about that first non-question I had put to him there in his living room and then, again, of how it had thrown him for such a loop.

"Honestly, I anticipated that you were some secret, CIA *boo-goo* from Fish and Wildlife come to pull me down. You know, a *boogie man.* It's really weird. People don't realize it, but when you go through something like that, you really do get paranoid. You do. It's a tough thing to fight. It's just one of the battles you have to put aside."

Kysar said it was only recently that he had come to feel more secure with the idea that the government really *wasn't* going to reopen his case and put him on trial.

"I think what people need to know is that, not that our government is a *bad* government, but that our government's a *human* government. It fails. It's better than anything in the world but, at the same time, it's got shortcomings. And it needs to be chastised sometimes to better itself."

There was that one question, though, that I never asked Kysar straight out—the one most other people always seemed to ask first. I think that by not asking it, by never broaching the subject myself, that it eventually became crucial to Kysar that I hear his answer to it.

The last time I spoke with him, he leaned into the matter himself by mentioning his one lingering regret, the one thing he still felt dishonest about. It was the answer he gave federal investigators way back when, for the very first time, somebody looked him dead in the face and asked if he knew he was shooting at a wolf that day just outside Yellowstone.

"That was the mistake I made. I should have told them up front the first time, I suspected the thing was a wolf. I didn't *know* it. But I suspected he was a wolf.

"I've run this through my head thousands of times— '*Did I* know *it was a wolf?*' No, I didn't. I absolutely did not *know* it was a wolf. I suspected. I *suspected* he was a wolf. But I had no way of *knowing* unless I shot him and looked at him.

"The bottom line is, I wasn't absolutely honest on this deal. I'm not sayin' that I was any different than anybody else. I was out to save my skin.

"When I said I thought it was a coyote, that wasn't the truth. It wasn't. But, at the same time, what do you do? What do you say when they tell you it's a hundred thousand dollar fine and a year in jail for shootin' a wolf. What are you gonna say? In the heat of the battle, when you've got law enforcement agents confiscatin' your film, interrogatin' you twice a day. How do you be *honest* with a government that makes you an outlaw? They tell you that there ain't nothin' up there like that, and then they put a hundred thousand dollar fine on it and a year in jail. What do you do?

"I'm tellin' you the honest to God, slobberin' truth right now. Yeah, I lied when I told 'em it was a coyote. I didn't know what else to tell 'em.

"The last conversation I had with a law enforcement officer, I was real tickled when he called me up and he said, '*You're off the hook, Jerry.*' He says, '*You're free and clear to go.*' But he said, '*I want to know one thing.*' He says, '*What did you see up there, Jerry?*'

"And I told him. I said, '*What I seen up there was four or five coyotes runnin' with that black wolf.*'

"And I said, '*I'll tell you somethin'.*' I said, '*Don't let anybody ever kid you. I don't care if you've never, ever, ever seen one in your life—once you've seen one, you* know *you've seen a wolf.*'

"And you know what he said?

"He said, '*I'll be damned,*' and he hung up on me. He said, '*I'll be damned,*' he hung up on me, and he pressed it no further than that. Absolute truth."

"I *knew* it was different. I knew it was different when it took off runnin' and I was grabbin' my rifle, pullin' it out of that scabbard and rollin' off my horse—and I wasn't the only one that was rollin' off my horse and grabbin' my rifle—the guy with me had his rifle out. . . . And he woulda shot, too. But I shot.

"And, shucks, I don't think either one of us probably could do it again in a thousand tries."

After all this time, over long-distance, Kysar was finally describing for me how the animal he had in his sights that day just outside Yellowstone ran with its tail straight out and its ears thrown forward.

"He *floated*. I'll tell you, until you've seen a wolf—there's something romantic about it and there's something that's very *wild*. It's something that pulls the spirit out deep within you. I know it does. When you see one of them things floatin' through the trees like that, it's just somethin' that grips the *wildness* inside you. It's some primitive deal. Don't ask me what it is. But there's somethin' very unique about a wolf runnin' through trees.

"I still stand by the fact that they're a hard animal to live with. What I'm sayin' is I'm *not* a wolf-lover. But there's somethin' wild about a wolf runnin' through trees like that.

"Anybody that's ever seen one *knows* they've seen one."

Like the man said. I'll be damned.

Tourist Country

I have a farm in Maine and I love the fact that there are bears and coyotes living in my woods. I very seldom see them, or even see signs of their presence, but I just like knowing that they are there, and would be very unhappy to learn that they had left. I would also not feel myself entirely compensated for the loss if some of my (artificial intelligence research) friends stocked my woods with lots of robot beasties, though the idea, if imagined in detail, is enchanting. It matters to me that there are wild creatures, descendants of wild creatures, living so close to me. Similarly, it delights me that there are concerts going on in the Boston area that I not only do not hear, but never even hear about.

—Daniel C. Dennett, *Consciousness Explained*, 1991

Artist Point

THREE TIMES THAT SUMMER I WENT LOOKING TO SPEND EQUAL time at the Defenders of Wildlife booth, which advocated wolf recovery in Yellowstone as much as Troy Mader opposed it, and three times I failed to find it. It was always described to me as stationed in a grassy, curbed area between the parking lot and asphalt walking paths that led to Artist Point just south of Canyon Village, maybe a five-minute drive from the very spot where Mader himself had chosen to hold forth for six weeks. Once, I spoke on the phone with one of the booth's organizers to get a sense of their general hours of operation and twice I cruised the lot at those times when I happened to be in the neighborhood anyway. On a third visit I found a parking space and waded among the other tourists for a couple hours on the off chance that a Defender or two might show and set up while I was off drinking in the spectacle, admiring the scent of pine and the occasional passing cigar. In the end, I decided to question neither the Defenders' resolve nor my own. I decided after three attempts, just as after three days of trying to catch and collar a timber wolf in Wisconsin, that I probably wasn't going to beat fate on this particular point for the rest of the summer.

I entertained myself through that final try, though, by watching people, by sitting on public benches and scribbling freely-associated thoughts about that name, Artist Point. Much later, I would read that the site was considered the most famous of the viewpoints on the south rim of the Grand Canyon of the Yellowstone River. F. Jay Haynes, an early park photographer, probably named the spot in about 1883, believing, as others have, that Thomas Moran had made sketches there for his 1872 painting of the canyon, rather than on the north side at what was now called Moran Point.

While I was sitting there, though, I decided Artist Point in Yellowstone was just like a slice of suburbia—for the most part, safe and warm. The slopes were deep and steep, but the walkways were explicitly marked with stone walls and safety rails. What I felt, on the whole, seemed as familiar to me as the observation deck high atop the Empire State Building back in Manhattan. There was no pretension toward understanding the full view since there was, clearly, too much for visitors to take in at once. So, instead, they grazed as they did at shopping malls, waiting in turn for their moment alone at the edge, lingering little, their expressions ranging from awestruck to irritated to those who would seem at a loss if they tried to guess what all the fuss was about. This place was an expression of modern America on vacation, I decided—the strict budgeting of time, expense, and distance traveled by the end of the day.

I heard a piercing whistle, then—

"Hey, Bob. Let's go."

"Mike, leave me alone. Don't touch me. Don't touch me. *Don't.*"

"You guys bring any extra batteries?"

"*Nuh-uh.* I was looking for some back in the store."

"Hey, Dad. There's a great picture over here."

Then, while I watched a couple clamber to stand and balance hand-in-hand on a bench to photograph themselves against a panorama above the heads of passersby, I asked a question of myself in capital letters and circled it twice—

JUST WHAT THE HELL WAS TOURISM LIKE IN AMERICA BEFORE CAMERAS AND HOME VIDEO?

I was already accustomed to finding myself wedged in traffic jams at the sighting of a single, hairy brown speck of a bear rummaging in the distance. One bison grazing five feet from the road, I knew full well, stopped traffic cold for hours. If it weren't for those bison, though—those prehistoric-looking creatures that are big enough and dully-stubborn enough to feed in the middle of the day in places where they could be seen from the roadsides when traffic was wholly gelatinous—I imagined many tourists might leave the park feeling gypped for not having captured an immediate, intimate wildlife experience of their own in Yellowstone. Early in my time in the park, I discovered quite by accident that you could fool other tourists into pulling over in droves just by stopping and gazing intently into the middle distance. They wanted to see what you saw and come away with a picture to prove it. That snapshot, I soon understood, was often as important to them as the experience that made it, that some lives didn't feel completely real unless they were fully-documented.

"Excuse me, mister, will you take our picture?" As a man sitting alone with an open notebook in such places for long stretches, I was often asked and, always, I obliged.

I am fortunate to have waited long enough that day to have any sense of smugness bowled over by the sublime. There arrived in time a blind man, balding and thin, with a red-tipped white cane and the company of two escorts, a woman and a young girl. They held his arms like family as he turned his ears to the falls rather than his eyes. He asked and they offered a description in murmurs and, as they spoke, he smiled. From that moment on, I have often wished I could have heard what made him smile so.

"*Oooooh, ooh*, the sun. You see the sun? Get the sun. Get a picture of the sun there on the falls. Did you see *that*? The sun right there in the middle on the top, just for a second, the sun. Did you see that? Did you get it?—*Here*, give me the camera."

Emigrant, Montana

SIX GENERATIONS OF PETE STORY'S KIN HAVE LIVED AND WORKED on a ranch in the Paradise Valley outside Emigrant, Montana, near milemarker 30 on highway 89 out of Yellowstone's north entrance at Gardiner. Story himself represented the fourth. His great grandfather came here a year after the Civil War on the Bozeman Trail with Montana's first herd of Texas longhorns and fifteen wagons of supplies for the region. It was the last civilian party to make it through, Story says, before Red Cloud shut it down. Story's people were here before Custer was defeated. They were here before there was a U.S. Forest Service or Department of Agriculture. They were here a good six years before that former Union commander Ulysses S. Grant signed a sizable chunk of land to the south into national servitude as Yellowstone National Park. These days, more than a 127 years later, Story told me, he rarely visited the park himself unless he had company or out-of-state relations to show around. He made it sound like he was a dissident living alongside the border of an unfriendly dominion, a man who was loath to set foot in the very place that distracted so much of his attention.

From a kitchen hallway deep inside a white, sprawling house hidden from the road below a canopy of cottonwood trees with trunks so craggy and vast one would have to stretch hard to reach an arm halfway around, Story shouldered open a door into what seemed a private chamber packed with ancient papers and artifacts. There wasn't space enough to flop a mattress down inside the walls and still have gaps to walk around, yet there was room enough to manage a desk and shelves yoked with heirlooms and personal effects. This was Story's modest family museum, I decided, a place where he probably drifted on occasion to get his bearings. He pointed out a spot on a map of the spread framed and mounted on the wall—

"That's where my great-grandpappy stood off Indians in 1866. Wasn't much of a fight. These people were mostly straight out the Confederate cavalry and they had lots of rifles and six guns. They were tough bastards, and the Indians turned around and left 'em alone."

The family now held title to 11,000 acres, Story said, far more than his great-grandfather ever had.

"The ranch has changed size with every generation. Just depends on whether we were flat-ass broke. It's expanded in good times and shrunk to beat hell in bad times. Everything human is cyclical. There's a thirty-year cow cycle. Every other generation gets burned so bad in the cow business that it's another generation before they get back in."

There were now about thirty people living on the ranch. One son ran the operation while another made a living as an outfitter. Story himself was recently retired, but certainly not mellowing, after making a career of twenty years in the Montana state legislature.

"After five terms it suddenly hit me. I was sitting and listening to the oratory and it struck me it was like endlessly repeating the third grade. So I traded down twenty years. I found a young man that thought the same way I did and I got him elected. He's proving to be a very excellent senator."

Story said he didn't miss his days at the capital in Helena in the least, that he *hated* government, actually. Always had. Always will.

"No, I don't trust government. I don't trust regulators or anyone else. Whenever government turns its hand to something, it usually makes it worse. There's a few shiny exceptions, of course. But you have to think long and hard to think of one.

"Government gets bound up in red tape. That's the short end of it.

"*Government*," Story said again with the emphasis of disdain. "I've dealt with five different bureaucracies and what I've found is that the motivation of the bureaucrat is to not let anything occur. The only way he can get canned is to make a decision.

"At least," he said, "now that I'm out of politics, *I* don't have to know everything."

That last remark I had a difficult time taking to heart. Story, I knew full well, was a cranky old man, because he had said as much himself. In the space of a few hours, he had already described himself as a *redneck* several times and, once, as something just shy of a *right-wing loony tune.*

"I'm *Politically-Incorrect* on all points. I'm a white, cattle-ranching Anglo Saxon. I'd be an *anarchist* if I weren't so square."

Story had looked me over good and hard when I arrived—up, down, all around. Like Tom Skeele, like Jerry Kysar, Story seemed highly-suspicious of me and my equivocal motives when I first darkened his porch door. While I sat in a chair he pulled out for me at one edge of his dining room table, Story circled round and asked me *twice* what I was doing out here, why I had come all this way from New York City—not just onto his land, mind you, but to the American West, *period.*

I stammered and took a shot. I began with lineage, something I guessed Story might respect.

I told him that both of my parents were raised on dirt farms next door in North Dakota, that my father was born there in 1931 during the Great Depression, at the outset of a famous decade of plagues of Biblical proportion—drought, dust, locusts, extreme cold, heat and hunger. I said my father had taken me back there several times when I was a kid, that he had driven me around the old place and told me about watching his father and other farmers bust rock and build roads by hand for the government because all their crops were dead and there was no other work. I said my father remembered eating lard when there was no other food, that he remembered killing gophers for a two-cent bounty the tails brought from the county—

Story cut me off.

While I thought I might score points with family farm legend, by Story's measure, apparently, pedigrees that only went back one generation were damn near worthless. So, since I had brought it up, he asked—turning, squinting, taking a seat right across from me—what about that last name? What about my *people*? Where had they had come from? What did they do for a living, you know, before they came to this country?

It struck me as a peculiar, personal line of questioning, but I tried to accommodate him. I tried to remember what I had been told, what my father had researched and written down with an illustrative family tree years earlier—that my paternal great grandfather, Johann, and his wife, Maria, had come here in 1896 from Old Postal, Bessarabia after he had served seven years conscription in the army of Czar Alexander I, fighting in some sort of pointless foreign intrigue in and around Vienna—that they were the descendants of Palatine Germans whose homeland was decimated three hundred years earlier by the Thirty Years' War—that for generations they had wandered and settled throughout Hungary, Poland, Germany and Bessarabia.

Beyond that, I didn't remember much, so, floundering, I told Story what my father, now a gray-haired Lutheran theologian in Ohio, had said to me when I first set out for the West in his red pick-up a month or so earlier. He told me that in such a time and place as his father and grandfathers knew, there was no room for notions of coexisting with wolves and wilderness. They were the instruments and outcome of evil works, and to think of them otherwise was a luxury that simply never had crossed their minds.

If Story was feeling any affinity for what I was trying to say it certainly didn't register on his face. I was beginning to think it had been a big mistake to admit roots in farming peasantry to a fourth-generation rancher, so I changed the subject. I said I personally first got curious about Yellowstone and the wolf issue specifically when I happened to read a wire-service article about Jerry Kysar the previous fall, that it happened to be around the time I attended a lecture at graduate school exploring Chekhov and Tolstoy's contrasting views on the question of *Nature v Culture*, how Tolstoy portrayed nature as romantic and grand and how Chekhov thought it would just as soon kill you as pay you any mind. Or, I said, running completely adrift of ideas with Story staring me in the face, that was the way I remembered it at least. To this day, I'm not sure if it was out of pity or disgust, but Story relented.

"Son," he said, "there are broader issues and then there are broader issues than the broader issues. *Nature versus Culture—that's* the bigger issue."

From that moment on, I'm sure, Story looked on me as pure greenhorn. That much was obvious. What he still seemed to have trouble sorting out, though, was just what color *green*.

A while later, when I asked how many head of cattle he ran, Story replied, as if I should have known better, that it was a *terribly* impolite question to ask of any rancher.

"If we did tell you we'd be like the Red Chinese, we'd be lying. That's like asking a man how much money he has in the bank."

What he offered, instead, was a tour of the place. He pushed his arms through the sleeves of a gray cotton jacket and yanked his head into a crisp shantung hat.

Then he told his wife Eileen, who had been puttering away at something in the kitchen, that he would check on the grandkids while he was out.

He had better, she said.

Eileen had taken a call earlier that afternoon from their son's house inquiring after two of the grandsons. Story had told me there were eight homes on the ranch. He said while the original was gone, the one in which we were standing was built in 1920 in the wild days of the ranch, so there was probably more booze in the foundation than water. His son's place was the newest, completed only a few years ago, only a few hundred yards away. When the call came, Story told his wife that, *yes*, he had given the boys tacit permission to go off shooting at the dump.

Eileen rolled eyes at him.

"You really should be with them," she said.

Story looked pained.

"He's *fourteen*," he said.

Eileen reminded him there was a younger boy along, too.

"Well, he's *ten*."

Minutes later, Story fulfilled his obligation by easing off the gas and hollering out the open window of his pick-up—"YOUR DAD IS HOME NOW."

The older boy waved, sort of, and replied—"Yeah, okay."

Story coasted and watched his grandson's aim but never stopped. Inside the truck, the radio roared as Story gunned the accelerator and dodged and plowed through craters in the road as large as bombshell explosions. As he negotiated the rise, he came to explain why we had to duck out of the house just then without attracting the notice of his lurking, and at-the-moment housebound, Great Dane. There were buffalo up where we were headed, Story said, and they sometimes kill dogs out of hand.

"He's a canine *idiot savant*. He can open any door that isn't locked in this valley. But he hardly has sense to wag his tail and walk at the same time."

Story said then that while he didn't remember much of what *his* father and grandfather actually said about wolves in their day, he did remember they always kept wolf hounds around the place.

"Wolf hounds can outrun wolves," Story said. "These were brave hounds. One man can knock a wolf down but you've got to find the son of a bitch first. Wolf hounds can do that.

"Now what we'll do on Story ranch, I'm sure, is maybe raise wolf hounds."

Story looked over at me, maybe to make sure I was listening, and repeated himself anyway.

"I suppose we're going to have to start running wolf hounds again."

When we reached a fence line, Story had me get out and open the gate. I think he wanted to see if I would botch the job of unfastening the post and walking a limp stretch of barbed-wire out of the way without getting run over. Or gored. I managed.

There was, indeed, a small herd of bison bunched and munching grass a few minute's drive away, six or seven of them, adults and calves alike. Story suspected two of the adults may have been bulls—which, he said, was one more than he needed. He watched their hindquarters closely the whole time we were there.

Story said they had bought the adults as calves the previous year since they were thought to be less inclined to bust open a fence and wander off. He made it sound like they were just trying these few out for size, just as an experiment, and I did get a sense they were living under something of a quarantine.

Bison weren't very popular in some corners of the West these days, in part, because ranchers have a dreaded fear of a disease they sometimes carry, *brucellosis*, which can cause spontaneous abortions in cattle. It is an exotic contagion, scientists say, brought to the Americas with imported domesticated stock. It infected native, free-ranging elk and bison herds that, in turn, were suspected of reinfecting ranchers' grazing stock from time to time. All told, the cattle industry and government agencies reportedly have spent on the order of $3.5 billion over the years to try to eradicate the disease. Some ranchers opposed wolf recovery because they thought wolves eating Yellowstone's widely-infected bison might carry brucellosis to cattle outside the park, that it might spread over the range, in part, through wolf scat. Some of the studies I had read recently suggested the contrary, though—that wolves' feisty digestive tracts may actually return fewer brucellosis agents to the soil than they eat.

Bison also weren't necessarily highly-regarded locally because of all they had come to symbolize across the West in recent years. Both the U.S. Department of the Interior and the National Park Service, for instance, featured bison on their departmental emblems. In December 1985, images bounced around the globe by satellite of hunters shooting Yellowstone bison as they crossed the park's northern boundary in search of winter forage. Containing the spread of brucellosis, again, was cited as the state's rationale for the cull. By 1990, when civilian hunters were replaced by professional sharpshooters, almost 700 of the park's dispersing bison had been dispatched in such public fashion.

Bison were also at the core of a dangerous idea first floated in 1987 by Frank and Deborah Popper, two professors at Rutgers University in New Jersey. They wanted to transform as much as one quarter of America's Great Plains—139,000 square miles spanning ten states—into the world's largest natural and historical preservation effort, an ecological reserve they would call the *Buffalo Commons.* The plan called for allowing at least 110 counties that were already economically-distressed and underpopulated to return to open prairie. There was more money to be made, more sensibly, from tourism, service industries and environmentally-sustainable commerce, the Poppers suggested, than by continuing to force a less-than-hospitable landscape into intensive, government-subsidized agriculture. Converts to the idea in Montana had recently come to call their corner of the proposed commons the *Big Open.* The seat of the reserve they planned along the eastern edge of the state, it turned out, would be a remote cowboy outpost called Jordan. Local reaction, reportedly, was not entirely enthusiastic.

There was also a movement afoot of late—championed by media moguls Ted Turner and Jane Fonda from their 130,000-acre *Flying D Ranch* near Bozeman, no less—to interest the red-meat-loving American consumer in bison products. The meat was leaner and better tasting, Turner claimed. The animal was thought to be better suited for harsh conditions, easier on fragile environments and water resources and the price, Turner argued—since money always carries influence—offered ranchers a higher profit margin.

"So these things, they look awkward as hell and they're stupid as hell," Story said. "But they're capable of taking care of themselves.

"This guy we got 'em from said if you go in a corral and you don't bring 'em food they don't understand. Said if the tail goes up and the head goes down, get the hell out of there."

Story elected to stay in the truck to watch the herd from a distance and that, I said, was just fine with me. He said he expected them all to get a little heavier and taller, that with all these choice eats, they should get just as big and ugly as any buffalo inside the park.

"You know," Story started again, "it certainly does look like we've got *two* bulls."

Story had me play with the gate again on the way out, but this time when I got back he had another map of the area flattened across the seat.

"The yellow is mine and we're right here," Story said. "All those in between sections are allotments. So we're checkerboarded with the Forest Service and they're treatin' us sort of like Saddam treats the Kurds."

Before I arrived at Story's ranch, I had read that something on the order of five million cows had grazed all of America's western range at the beginning of the grand old days of ranching around 1870. Less than fourteen years later, the number peaked somewhere between thirty-five to forty million. There were reports of droughts and massive die-offs of cattle, however, during the 1880s and 1890s. One account claimed there were so many rotting carcasses throughout the West back then that a traveler could throw rocks from one dead animal to the next.

These days, more than half the earth's solid ground is said to be grazed by domestic animals. In the American West, the proportion is closer to 70 percent. In sixteen states alone, the federal government leases to ranchers and farmers for livestock grazing more than 300 million acres, an area the size of the eastern seaboard from Maine to Florida. All told, there are more than 30,000 federal grazing allotments nationwide—varying in size from forty acres to more than a million—and more than 24,000 permittees. A third of all ranchers in eleven western states reportedly use public land at least part of the year. Livestock graze almost 80 percent of public land managed by the U.S. Department of Agriculture and the Bureau of Land Management in the U.S. Department of the Interior. Grazing allotments were included in about half the nation's designated wilderness areas, 35 percent of wildlife refuges and a quarter of the space in national parks, monuments, memorials, recreation and historic areas. No grazing is allowed either inside Yellowstone or on 7.5 million acres of government forest on its boundaries. Cows do, however, graze 8 percent of Yellowstone's sister park to the south, Grand Teton National Park, and between 14 and 71 percent of the six national forests in the area.

Scientists say that nowadays it takes something like 4.8 kilograms of grain and 3,000 liters of water to produce a single kilogram of beef in America. What that translates into actual acreage depends on the land. While one acre can support a cow in Georgia, for instance, a similar cow in the arid West needs upwards of thirty acres. In 1990, federal agencies reportedly spent at least $52 million more on programs dealing specifically with livestock—pipelines, fencing, water tanks and range management—than they collected in grazing fees. Word of the disparity fueled a label for public-lands grazing that independent-minded cowmen like Story found particularly offensive—*welfare ranching*. By the summer of 1993, the grazing fee on public land throughout America was still less than two dollars per cow per month. Private land leases were typically three to four times higher. The government makes allotments based on AUMs, or Animal Unit Month, the amount of forage required to feed a cow, a cow and her calf, or two yearlings for thirty days. While allotments can't be owned technically, they are tied loosely to private property rights. Permits are often inherited, although less than 15 percent of allotments these days remain with the families to whom they were originally permitted. The value of allotments is taxed by the Internal Revenue Service and recognized as collateral by banks. That summer, I heard ranching advocates regularly cite the government's original intention to give away or sell almost all the territory it acquired through conquest or Manifest Destiny, that this land was always meant to remain available to local economies and entrepreneurs. By and large, most of the ranchers I met that summer saw grazing on public land as their right rather than a privilege. If an allotment wasn't used, current laws obliged the government to take it away and give it to somebody else.

When I asked, Story said he would much rather own the white squares on this map outright than lease them with a permit. He said he had tried for twenty years to buy them, but even with all his old pull up in Helena, the government refused.

"Any proposals I made, even if they liked 'em, it took 'em ten years to respond," Story said. "Them people are a bunch of *flibberty gibbets*.

"Government really doesn't understand what makes agriculture tick. This place, if the dollar were the bottom line, I'd have sold out years ago. In this area, land is selling for four or five thousand dollars an acre right now—and I've got eleven thousand of it.

"Anywhere in the country, good year or bad, good operator or bad, any rancher or farmer could sell out and put his money in anything, passbook savings, and make more than he's making at ranching.

"What's keeping him in ranching is his attitude, and if government destroys that attitude," Story said, "this country will *starve*.

"It won't be because we've paved over too many farms and made them into K-Marts or shopping malls or freeways. It'll be because the tax policy and the regulation policy discouraged us from staying in business.

"The greatest danger to your alimentary canal right now is government," Story said. "The honest-to-God truth is that the worst threat to your health, to your eating habits, to your housing ability, is mistaken government policy by people who think government is the answer to everything. And a government that intrudes into every facet of human existence."

Story got out of the truck cab, walked a pace or two away and called me over to follow more closely the things he was pointing out in sweeping gestures all across the valley.

"Now, what I'm showing you, you can see some green, but you also on all of these hills, in all directions, see the yellow. Not the bright yellow, the bright yellow is sweet clover. I'm talking about the other brown that's all over those lower hills and all over my hill here.

"See?

"Now what that is, everywhere you look in this country there is *old* grass. When you're in Yellowstone all you'll see is *green* grass. You'll see no *old* grass. They've *et* it to the ground."

Rangeland in America is typically classified as areas unsuitable for intensive cultivation or forestry. It's dry, rough, hot and cold usually with poor drainage and shallow soil. Around Yellowstone, where temperatures range as high as a hundred degrees in summer and as low as sixty below in winter, there is usually less than twelve inches of precipitation a year. In the mountains, and there are plenty, as much as 85 percent of annual precipitation comes in the form of snow. Ideally, when cows graze these parts, they should be allowed to stay and eat only one course, long enough to stimulate plant growth with intense pruning, but not long enough to take the second bite that might damage root systems before a plant has a chance to recover. When perennial native grasses are overgrazed, annual weeds and tough shrubs such as cheatgrass, tumbleweed, sage and mesquite have a tendency to spread. This new, less-diverse plant community is more vulnerable to erosion—so, ultimately, watertables diminish and there is less food and drink to go around for livestock and wildlife alike.

There was a growing awareness these days, though, that no grazing whatsoever could be just as damaging to the range as overgrazing. The trampling effect of hooves— what used to be accomplished by giant herds of wild ungulates before cows arrived—is needed to break soil and establish new seeds in brittle environment. Cows stomp up decomposing material that may otherwise choke and inhibit photosynthesis. Their waste contributes to a carbon cycle that promotes plant biodiversity.

To stay in business and protect his resource these days, a rancher in the New West was expected to climb off his horse, crawl around the ground on hands and knees and, essentially, develop skills of an open range *maitre d'*— juggling time, numbers of consumers and a willingness to shoo the overflow off to other pastures.

Yellowstone, however, said Story, had failed to heed that approach when it came to protecting its own *precious* resource. He pointed again.

"All of our creeks in this valley, there's willow thickets along the creeks. You won't find *that* in the park."

They were all long gone, Story said, eaten into oblivion by all the elk running around Yellowstone.

"That *park.* Our *government.* It's the worst case of overgrazing that you will ever see anywhere, is this Yellowstone *Park.* This is the government that wants to tell us how to handle *our* affairs.

"They dither about everything. But they're their own worst enemies. What they've done to the park themselves with overgrazing and natural burns—it's *bullshit.*

"The wildlife threat isn't from *development.* The animals can put up with that," Story said. "The threat is that the park will let them overgraze and become diseased and won't cull them properly.

"This new religion is that whatever nature does is *good.* Forest fires are *good* but logging is *bad,* and so forth.

"*This* is what we have to put up with.

"See, the first thing you were taught in school about nature was actually a hundred and eighty percent out. You were told that man was interfering with the balance of nature.

"But nature has *never* been in balance. There's *never* been a pristine state of nature that always stays the way it is. If predators' numbers go down, the herbivores increase. Then predator numbers go up and continue rising.

"What's going to happen in the park is they're going to graze it down to nothing. There'll be a bad winter, there'll be a tremendous die off and most of the park elk will be down here.

"But on our place we *do* control numbers. When we have too many, we let enough hunters in to take care of the excess. We have enough heavily-armed men up here every fall to retake Beirut. But we don't let 'em hunt moose, which is scarce, or bears, which is scarce, or mountain lions. We're overpopulated with elk and deer. So we let 'em take all they want of that."

Story seemed to head back toward the truck but wound up wandering even further afield.

"On this ranch we probably have four hundred elk and maybe four hundred deer. We also have wolverines in the mountain tops up here, and down along the river we have freshwater otter."

Story said there were probably eight mountain lions in the mountains around us and each probably brought down an elk a week. He said if I wanted, his grandkids could probably show me a black bear walking around his land. They were easier to find here, he said, than inside Yellowstone.

"Only our bears are *polite*," Story said. "When you see them they're *leaving* and this is because I shoot past them most of the time. I don't permit people to hunt bears on this ranch. But if I had a problem bear I'd make a rug out of it. The only bear I ever killed I'm sure was a park bear. He was tipping over my trash barrel out here, when I tipped him over. The park bears have a different attitude towards people.

"We do have coyotes, too. We thin 'em. We pop one anytime these tired old eyes can get one in their sights. But we're not going to wipe out the coyotes."

Story said he once saw a mess of coyotes chewing on a calf as it was being born. He said they had run the mother until she couldn't stand anymore—

"They weren't hurting *her*, but they were eating the calf as it came out. That's when I popped *them*.

"Eagles will also eat calves sometimes. If there's a calf left alone, an eagle will get it. The golden eagle up here lives in the mountains in the summer and the lower reaches in the winter, and eats deer. We've come across them having pulled a doe and a fawn down."

So obviously, Story said after completing his version of an ecological summary, he wasn't opposed to the idea of predators around his cows.

"The *wolf* is just the wrong animal. Chances are the wolves will abandon the park and follow the elk on down here and work on the livestock."

Story said he was convinced the government had already tried and failed, many times, to reintroduce wolves secretly to Yellowstone. He said he actually saw one of the animals himself some twelve years earlier.

"There's no mistaking it," Story said. "The last time they tried a transplant was in the late '70s. They won't admit that they tried to transplant them then. But there he was and I know damn well what I was looking at. He was up above the Gibbon Falls and I was just driving along and he was standing there about a hundred yards off the road lookin' at me. There were enough distinguishing features between a wolf and a coyote. I knew what I was lookin' at."

This animal was black, Story said, and big.

"This thing was upwards of a hundred pounds probably. I was just driving along and it stood there and watched me."

Later, I told Story that it sounded to me like he was already resigned to the idea of seeing an official wolf reintroduction program in Yellowstone someday.

"Oh, I think they're going to ram it through," he said.

"We know they're damaging to us. We know they won't stay in the park. We know, in fact, that as soon as they eat a little girl in the park that they'll want to get rid of the sons of bitches and then *we'll* have the problem."

All day, Story had scoffed at reports from Minnesota and northern Montana that suggested wolves killed less than one in 10,000 cows available to them. All day, Story was angered by statistics that claimed tourism and service industries had far supplanted ranching as the most significant aspect of his regional economy.

"This is *bullshit*," Story said. "They're not doing this for *tourists*. They're doing this to turn the whole state into a nice little playground for *themselves*."

Story said while the conservationist movement itself was needed, maybe even necessary, in its early years, it had recently turned pernicious.

"Right now, most of the groups that call themselves environmental groups are headed by people who are environmental *thuggies*. They're not *pro-nature* so much as they are *anti-man*."

Story took me back down to the house one last time, to show me an Earth First! newsletter he had picked up in Seattle three or four years earlier and, in particular, an article with a headline that read—*Shooting Cows A Novel Idea.*

"They're plumb serious," Story said. "They spike trees and kill loggers. I presume they're serious."

He showed me other articles that suggested the biggest threat to the planet these days had come to be the birth rate of white middle class children.

"These people, their ultimate goal is to bring down society. By their own words," Story said. "You're getting *pseudo-science.* You're getting propaganda.

"They want to lock up the land and the wolf is their prime symbol," Story said. "But it isn't their *love* for the wolf so much as it's their *hate* for western civilization. You show me a wolf lover and I'll show you a *sociopath.*

"These *pro-wolf* people, aside from being sociopaths, they're *liars.* They're tremendous liars. They say the wolf won't hurt anything. The wolf is shy. Afraid of people. Hunts at night.

"Now, coyotes attack people. Mountain lions attack people. Bears attack people. Yet they're telling us that this bigger, more ferocious animal is going to be a pussycat. That's *silly.*

"You've got a real serious situation. The wolf is just one of the symptoms. And, in fact, we'll take care of our wolf problems. We'll be lawbreakers," Story said. "But it's not smart for a government to make most of its people lawbreakers. When you are by necessity forced to break one law, it makes it far easier to ignore all laws."

Early in our visit, Story had urged me to read one of his favorite books—Alston Chase's *Playing God In Yellowstone: The Destruction Of America's First National Park.* Story said the book, in short, ascribed most of the environmental problems in modern Yellowstone to more than a century of government mismanagement, incompetence, misguided science and political chicanery. When I told Story I had already read the book while I was traveling in Minnesota, he called out to Eileen in the kitchen to get the author himself on the phone, so I could make an appointment to meet him later in the week. Chase, it turned out, was one of Story's neighbors. He lived on the other side of the valley, about ten or fifteen miles up the road.

Chase, it also turned out, never let me inside his house. We talked for about an hour a few days later, sitting in the cold sun of his yard on the shoulder of a mountain while his two dogs, Daisy and Panda, cast about in electronic collars tuned to an underground network of invisible fencing. While Daisy growled continuously into my microphone, the conversation came to a standstill but once that afternoon, as we all turned to watch a doe with two fawns crossing an adjoining meadow.

At the time, Chase was taking a break from writing the latest of his syndicated columns. He had a regular audience of something on the order of 40 million readers in 150 newspapers across the country. He also served as a contributing editor to travel magazines, as a consultant to public television documentaries and, occasionally, as a university lecturer—at Harvard, Yale and Stanford, where, in some cases, his work was required reading. Chase told me he actually considered himself an academic first and foremost, that he would prefer to be remembered someday as a scholar who wrote about the philosophy of science. By the time I met him he already had published three books and a fourth was forthcoming about the nation's old-growth forests.

Playing God In Yellowstone, first published in 1986 when Chase was 51 years old, however, had thus far generated the most intense personal and professional firestorm of his career. In it, Chase wrote, among other things, that the ecological management strategy known as *natural regulation* was little more than a framework of convenience bent on advancing the political agendas of both the Park Service and the environmental movement. Scientists and researchers who explored ideas contrary to prevailing policy, Chase wrote, quite often were ignored and, in a very real sense, cast out of the professional loop.

Chase told me he himself received similar treatment after the book was published. He was booted out of his post as chairman of the Yellowstone Association, the park's non-profit natural history and science outreach program, and was soon branded as something of a pariah in the environmental community. Once, Chase said, he was described in the *Washington Post* by a reporter who had never met him as "a local curmudgeon who clearly likes to annoy the Park Service."

In the meantime, Chase said, his book was widely embraced by conservative Republicans and Libertarians as a handy indictment of federal bureaucracy, incompetence and waste even though, privately, Chase himself had always had the leanings of a Democrat. All his life, he told me, he had either voted for Democrats or he just plain hadn't voted.

"But the free-market types *loved* the book—for the wrong reasons, mind you. They took it as an argument for *privatizing* the park, which I don't agree with at all."

Still, Chase said, the book sparked more than a hundred reviews and articles across the country, including the cover of *Newsweek*. Environmental groups and their media, however, apparently decided the book didn't exist.

"Which was, under the circumstances, very *odd*. The book was more *right* than I had ever expected it to be. I really had expected and hoped that there would be more dialogue. And there was *none*. The fact is that the book raised some fundamental questions that they *don't* want to discuss."

Chase said he really hadn't involved himself much in the current controversy over wolf recovery in Yellowstone, that he had only received the full text of that summer's DEIS the previous Monday.

"But I *am* in favor of wolves coming back. I always have been because they were taken out illegally and secretly. So it's a moral and legal issue to me. It's a matter of simple justice."

Chase said he was troubled, however, by a number of inconsistencies he heard in arguments supporting the proposal. Among the most obvious was that the specific gray wolf subspecies that used to roam Yellowstone, *Canis lupus irremotus*, was probably long-since extinct. He said environmentalists, who usually split hairs about the subtle distinctions between such creatures as northern spotted owls and California spotted owls, for instance, were changing their approach to suggest that there actually isn't much difference between subspecies and that importing exotic wolves to the park from Canada was entirely acceptable.

Chase said he was troubled as well by assumptions that wolf recovery in Yellowstone somehow fit into Park Service *natural regulation* management strategies.

"Environmentalists have completely ignored the elk problem. Suddenly, when the wolves come along, they say as an argument, '*We've got to have wolves to take care of the elk.*' When they talk about wolf recovery they suddenly admit that there's an elk problem and I'm thinking, why is it only now that they think it's important?

"The assumption is being made that the wolves are going to help bring everything into some kind of natural equilibrium—which is basically bullshit.

"They think that the wolf is going to pull their chestnuts out of the fire on this problem. But it's *not*. There's no biologist anywhere who believes that wolves will ever make a significant dent in the elk population in Yellowstone. If there *were* sufficient numbers of wolves to have some kind of controlling impact on elk numbers, there would be so many wolves that when the elk numbers did come down eventually the ranchers really *would* be right. There really *would* be massive predation on livestock.

"You can't have it both ways," Chase said. "If there are going to be enough wolves to do a job on the elk, there are going to be enough wolves eventually to do a job on livestock.

"With respect to the current wolf reintroduction plan there's a lot of wishful thinking going on. In my view, what this shows is we have everything upside down. First of all, we talk about *ecosystem* management and nobody's practicing it. Everybody's practicing *species* management.

"What needs to be done is to bring the existing populations of large mammals in Yellowstone into a rough equilibrium *before* you reintroduce wolves. Get the elk numbers down to *one-tenth* of what they are today. Let the mule deer come back. Let the white-tail deer come back. Let the riparian areas regenerate. Let a lot of the other small mammals, rabbits, skunks and so on, become more abundant. *Then* reintroduce the wolves. That way it will stand a chance of succeeding.

"Yellowstone is a desert so far as small mammals are concerned. There's virtually no beaver left, no skunks and porcupines. Compared to the rest of Montana, there's very, very little because the *biomass* is almost completely taken up by the elk. So if wolves are put in the park and they're expected to do some *prey-switching*, they just couldn't do it."

I mentioned that some conservationists weren't entirely happy that the DEIS planed to designate wolves in the area as an *experimental population* rather than a fully-protected endangered species.

"There has to be flexibility built into the application of the Endangered Species Act," Chase said. "It was intended by the people who wrote the act. If conservationists continue insisting on the most extreme and literal interpretation of the Act, one of two things will happen. Either there will be massive economic dislocations and personal tragedies—on the part of blue-collar people mostly—or there will be an enormous political backlash that will ultimately do more damage to the Act than good.

"Common sense has to prevail. There's got to be some flexibility built into the system.

"From a personal standpoint," he said, "I'd love to think that there were wolves back up in those hills. But I also have a moral problem with saying to my neighbor across the road, '*You're going to have to have a certain number of cattle killed by wolves every year because I like to have wolves.'"*

Programs to compensate ranchers for livestock losses have to be spelled out at the outset, Chase said, adding that they ought to be financed neither by private environmental groups, as was being discussed at present, nor by U.S. taxpayers at large. The cost of wolf recovery, he suggested, would be paid more justifiably with some form of *user fee* on those who actually use the park. Outdoor recreation, in his opinion, was already too heavily subsidized by the government.

"Basically, it's an upper-middle class *entitlement.*"

He rattled off a series of statistics then from memory—*80 percent of black Americans have never visited a national park—80 percent of people who live in cities have never visited a park—the annual mean income of individuals in the United States is $23,000—the mean income of ranchers is $28,000—the mean income of visitors to national parks is $50,000—86 percent of the cost of running parks at present is subsidized by taxpayers—each individual wilderness visit is subsidized an average of $28 a day.*

"So you really have a *class* thing going on here," Chase said, "and I find that *ugly.*

"I have no problem with ending subsidies for grazing and ending subsidies for timber if we also end subsidies for recreation and everybody pays their own way."

"I guess if I were to come to a bottom line on this, I'd say that anybody who claims to know, or even to be able to make a reasonable guess as to whether wolf recovery will be successful in Yellowstone, both biologically and politically," Chase said, "is talking straight into their hats. Because *nobody* really knows."

Jackson, Wyoming

ON ONE OF THE SEVERAL OCCASIONS I CAME TO SPEND TIME WITH Norm Bishop that summer, we were rolling through Yellowstone's secluded Lamar Valley in his car one bright morning, he was talking as usual about politics and wolf whatnot, when he interrupted himself mid-sentence and waved a wiry finger toward a throng of bulky brown figures grazing nearby, so slowly.

"*Ahhhhhh*—look at the bison," Bishop said, always the park ranger, always the enthusiastic wildlife interpreter. Without prompting, he said Yellowstone's bison were actually hybrid descendants of the plains bison and the park's native mountain bison that were hunted to near extinction in the late 1800s. The animals we were looking at were part of the last free-ranging bison herd in North America. While as many as sixty million animals once roamed the Great Plains, they had been slaughtered indiscriminately, in part, to drive Native Americans off the land and make room for farming and ranching. These days, Bishop said, Yellowstone's population seemed to take after the park's native herd, migrating in bands of between ten to 400 animals at once.

"They're always on the move, you know. You hardly notice it because they look sort of static. But if, say, you sit down and eat lunch and you're watching them you notice that the whole business is just sort of in *motion*. It's fun to see. So they just don't stand there. They're always just sort of moving along."

You don't want to picnic *too* close, though, Bishop said—always the ranger, always dishing out safety tips and anecdotes about the possible consequences of horsing around with the great outdoors.

"There were a bunch of people standing around an elk cow in Mammoth the other day—my wife saw it—and they were within five or six feet of it and she was *really* giving them body signals that they'd better move back. She was *lunging* at them every once in a while and the people would jump back just a foot or two and then laugh. Like it was a *game*.

"She could have driven one of them *into the dirt*."

I mentioned a report of a tourist taunting a bison into a goring the previous week.

"Well, you know, with three million *do-dos* running around the park," Bishop started, then stopped himself. "Well, no, let me put it this way. My professor once said that any time you have twelve people together one of them will be a fool. And so when you have three million people in a park, one out of twelve, or some proportion like that, is going to be a fool and walk up and try to grab 'em by the horn and get an *eyeball-nose-nostril* shot with his 35mm wide-angle lens.

"*Ridiculous*."

Bishop, I had sensed even before I met him, had talents exquisitely suited for his job. He was the man the Park Service's top brass in Washington had hand-picked for the delicate and demanding task of leading Yellowstone's information and education programs about wolf recovery. For more than a decade, Bishop encouraged, and probably scripted, most all of the park's slide shows and campfire talks about wolves, including, I assumed, the presentation I had attended at Old Faithful. He handled the thousands of inquiries each year about Yellowstone wolf recovery from students, citizens and media people—including mine, since I happened to represent all three. As a consequence, I decided Bishop probably had the single largest postage and photocopying tab in all of Yellowstone. He kept a fancy shelf at his office with upwards of four dozen pigeon holes for all of the notable and topical reports, newsletters, digests and scientific studies he mailed to people all over the globe, replenishing each stack with a minimum run of 200 at a time. Each letter and phone message got his personal attention and treatment. He carefully discerned their level of interest, how deep they really wanted to go, then shipped off an appropriate, and usually generous, bundle of accumulated research and expertise.

In person, I found Bishop to act much the same way. When you asked him a question, his first reflex seemed to be to cite from memory an apt passage from a study, poll or historical reference, and then follow up with the context and perspective of personal experience. It wasn't that he liked to bury inquiries with particulars, necessarily. He just seemed to believe firmly that the answer to most anything could be found by researching, reviewing and sharing information with anybody who asked. He spoke plainly, in tones that rose out the top of his throat, maybe like a bluegrass singer, like a funny, charismatic, old codger using words like *gosh* with all sincerity. Not once, though, did I sense that Bishop ever believed in simple, pat answers. He carried the candor of tenure about him, that some things simply had to be said, that he was just the man to say them, the way only he could say them. A mutual acquaintance, an independent wildlife biologist, once joked that Bishop had been trying to retire for the last couple of years but he knew very well he wouldn't until wolves were back inside Yellowstone—that Bishop, in his heart, wanted to see this deal done sooner rather than later.

Bishop himself once shared with me a beef he has with media people—myself included, most likely—about how they cover the publication of serious reports like the DEIS by leafing through the executive summary—

"And then they'll go down to a barstool somewhere and stick a mike in somebody's face and if he says something else, then it's a *fifty-fifty* argument.

"One side of it is *this*, even though it may be a hundred studies, the other side of it's *this*, even though the guy maybe speaking completely through his hat.

"When I become a private citizen and a non-government person I think I'm going to start writing editorials about that to the papers and TV stations. Saying—'*Hey, folks. Come on. When you've got some data, tell us it's data. If you've got a barstool opinion, tell us it's a barstool opinion.*' Don't give us this fifty-fifty nonsense, that you're being fair to both sides of an issue by putting a *barstool* up against ten thousand *biologists*.

"*T'ain't* so," Bishop said. "That's one of my many little points of irritation about this whole thing."

Over time, while I watched him work at seminars and speaking engagements that summer, I noticed that Bishop often bristled when he heard someone in the audience suggest that the government's chief motivation for wolf recovery in Yellowstone was to create jobs for scientists. Bishop said that when he first transferred to Yellowstone ten years before, the research division had a staff of two scientists, a clerk and a technician working on something like eighty separate studies. These days, the Yellowstone Center for Resources houses about sixty people working on more than 300 research projects throughout the park.

"We *don't* need wolves to have research in Yellowstone. But the presence of wolves, getting them back, will give an *immense* opportunity for new knowledge about wolves and also about restoring extirpated species. That's going to be important because there are large carnivorous species that have been eliminated from places all over the world that now exist only in zoos."

There's an enormous difference between studying the recovery of more solitary animals, like grizzlies and mountain lions, Bishop explained, than of a highly-social animal like the wolf.

"The world is going to learn an awful lot about how to restore a species that has been eliminated from what happens here. It's going to *rewrite* the book on what we know about wolves."

Bishop, likewise, often seemed to have little patience for suggestions that wolf recovery was being imposed on Yellowstone and its neighbors by a bunch of bureaucrats and eco-bunnies back East. Invariably, he would start out by conceding to his audience that the greatest support for wolf recovery did come from the national level, citing, for instance, a 1989 poll of park visitors in which 74.2 percent of the respondents said they supported wolf reintroduction.

"Yellowstone is a national icon. It's a place that people all over the country feel is theirs."

Bishop would then cite polls that found majority support for wolf recovery even in the three states surrounding the park—Idaho, 67 percent, Montana, 52 percent, and Wyoming, 58 percent.

Once, in a more private setting, he added, "The local guys love to say—'*Well, it's all those easterners that want to put wolves in Yellowstone.*' That's a bunch of *bullshit*—it's total *bullshit*."

On another occasion, Bishop said it never ceased to amaze him how many opponents to wolf recovery often shared a mindset that separated the animal from all other forms of wildlife.

"In short, the rest of the earth was created by *God* and wolves were created by the *Devil.*

"*Gosh,*" Bishop said, "that goes back a long way in northern European cultures, back to where we're projecting our own worst traits onto wolves and then punishing *them* for it."

The last time I heard Bishop speak was at a one-day seminar he led in August at the Teton Science School in the mountains outside Jackson Hole. Near the end, I saw a young woman raise a hand and tell Bishop she wasn't sure it was fair to reintroduce wolves to a place that was still as contentious as Yellowstone. It was the one time I believe I saw Bishop smile to acknowledge the difficulty of addressing a remark before responding.

"All the questions about wolves and Yellowstone really boil down to just one. Are we *willing* to share the earth with another top predator?

"The reason that wolves belong in Yellowstone, and the justification for disrupting the lives of some wolves in Canada to bring them down here is, in part, because those wolves are going to have a short life in Canada anyway.

"It's a tough way of making a living, being a wolf. It's not as though wolves are living in a *cushy* place now and we're going to bring them into a *hostile* place. They're coming to another place which is probably no more or no less hostile than anywhere else wolves live."

In one study in Alaska, Bishop said, biologists X-rayed the skeletons of dead wolves and found them to be, by way of analogy, as bad off as rodeo cowboys. There were lots of bone breaks and injuries improperly healed from fights with competitors and kicks from prey. While captive wolves may have a life-span as long as twelve years, Bishop said, wild wolves usually only live through seven years, if they make it past high mortality rates first as pups, then as yearlings vying for precious little space in a pack hierarchy.

"But why they should be back in Yellowstone and why the proponents feel that it's justifiable to upset families of wolves and bring them down is that—*one*, Yellowstone is a great place for wolves, and—*two*, it's the only place in the Lower Forty-eight where if we restore wolves we'll have a complete component of all the significant fauna that was present when Europeans first came to the continent.

"That's important aesthetically. It's important historically. It's important biologically. So what we're trying to do in restoring wolves to Yellowstone is to restore a naturally-functioning ecosystem in the absence of one of the prime predators in that ecosystem. The ecosystem is short. It's incomplete. In Yellowstone, we have a highly-attuned ecosystem in which one of the spark plugs is missing, and that's the wolf."

Bishop, whom I found partial to quoting the early conservationist Aldo Leopold, then closed his response with Leopold's remark that relegating wilderness to Alaska, where there's lots of it, is something like relegating happiness to heaven—

"Some of us may never get there."

Buffalo Ranch

NORM BISHOP WAS IN ATTENDANCE AT ONE OF THE OTHER WOLF recovery seminars I attended that summer, this time a three-day stint taught by John Weaver at the Yellowstone Institute. The Institute had been established on the site of the park's historic Buffalo Ranch in the Lamar Valley, in buildings and cabins where early park rangers once stayed as they herded plains bison to breed with and supplement the park's near-extinct population of native mountain bison. In recent years, Weaver's class here had developed a reputation as something of an annual wolf summit. In 1987, the same year that the national president of Defenders of Wildlife took the class, Congressman Wayne Owens of Utah attended and, on the spot, hired Tim Kaminski, one of Weaver's assistants, to return to Washington to lobby and draft legislation on behalf of wolf recovery. Kaminski stayed in Washington for two years, Weaver said, and would be back as an assistant in the class again this year.

Among the other attending guest speakers, aside from Bishop, would be Renee Askins, leader of the Wolf Fund based in Moose, Wyoming, and two members of her staff. Askins, too, used to work for Weaver as an assistant about ten years earlier. She had since gone on to become among the most outspoken and well-recognized advocates of wolf recovery in Yellowstone. Her group was dedicated solely to that purpose, she always said. Once wolves were recovered in the park, the Wolf Fund would declare victory in a sense by shutting its doors and closing down for good. Through the years, Askins had spread the message by getting herself quoted and profiled in print media ranging from the *Jackson Hole Guide* to *The New York Times*, *LIFE* and *People* magazines. She had been interviewed on national television by Larry King and Charlie Rose. She courted corporate funding from companies like Patagonia and wooed the celebrity appeal of such luminaries as Robert Redford, whose voice could be heard narrating the outgoing message on the Wolf Fund's answering machine. Askins, simply, was someone who could make things happen.

"The wolf is a species that comes to us with a certain amount of cultural baggage," Weaver said as he greeted the class the first day. "By that I mean that people don't generally view wolves the same way they do other types of wildlife. People have very emotional feelings about wolves either *pro* or *con*.

"I readily admit that I have a certain perspective that I'll be sharing with you."

Weaver himself was the first person the government hired to check out reports of wolf sightings throughout the park back in 1975. While there was talk already of wolf reintroduction back then, there was also that lingering question of whether it was even necessary. Somebody had to be the first to look into the possibility that wolves could still be hanging around the park from long ago or, perhaps, returning on their own anew.

"I spent two years on it," Weaver said. "Twelve months in the field over a period of two years, all seasons of the year. I found evidence of one wolf and it was over here in Sunlight Basin. I found tracks of the animal on two different occasions and I had it howl back in response to some tape-recorded howlings one morning.

"I am *confident* it was a wolf."

(I might mention—just as a personal observation, not as a sign of disrespect—that one of the first things I noticed about Weaver was he pronounced *coyote* both ways, as two-and three-syllable words, and that he also, on occasion, said *wooof* rather than *wolf*.)

In 1978, when Weaver published his findings in *The Wolves of Yellowstone*, he recommended the active restoration of the species to Yellowstone in formal terms— because it was a major missing link in the ecosystem— because it was a native animal absent due to human actions—and because the idea was biologically and ethically sound.

To this day, he remained one in the so-called *Delphi Group* of fifteen North American wolf experts that the Park Service consulted about wolf recovery. Professionally, at present, he was in the throes of data analysis and the write up of his doctoral dissertation at the University of Montana based on a three-year study of wolf ecology at Jasper Park in Alberta, Canada.

"It's an area that is very similar to Yellowstone. That's why I chose to work there," Weaver said. "Before I went up to Jasper I had a *textbook* knowledge of how far wolves travel. After working up there for three years I have an *on-the-ground* knowledge of how far wolves travel.

"It's one of the *essences* of this species."

Weaver likes to teach in the field, to take his students to see some of the very things he would be talking about. On the first day, the first such outing we took as a group was to a small plateau with a view of the Lamar River not far from Soda Butte. It required, however, that we walk— briskly, to keep up with Weaver—across a deceptively-vast field below, sinking at times up to our calves in marshy, sucking mud, hefting above us the weight of canteens, camera bags, daypacks and our brand-new, standard-issue, bright orange three-ring binders chock full of university studies, government reports, clippings from scientific journals and other small-print, double-sided course materials Weaver had photocopied for our reference. There was a great deal of quiet uncertainty expressed among the students in the early going about whether we really *wouldn't* be quizzed on all of it in the end. Only Bishop, I decided, might have passed.

"It's like a *serengeti* up here," Weaver said once we arrived. "We're talking about heaven for wolves right here. You're looking at the heart of wolf country in Yellowstone."

All told, Weaver said, there were about 100,000 ungulates, or hooved mammals, residing in the ecosystem. The bulk of these were elk, about 51,000, an all-time high. As many as 20,000 elk lived within park boundaries year round and were never subject to hunting.

"I'm not sure I can think of any other place in North America where you have that amount of ungulates that are not subject to some sort of hunting."

On lands surrounding the park, Weaver said, hunters took an average of 14,000 ungulates a year, or about 15 percent of the total.

"Once you get to a fully-recovered wolf population of a hundred animals, say, they're going to take between a thousand and twelve hundred ungulates per year—about one percent. So even with a fully-recovered population of wolves in Yellowstone, hunters are going to be taking seven to eight times as many as what the wolves are."

The DEIS projected that wolf recovery might require the reduction of only the harvest of moose in a few areas outside the park. Weaver said it would amount to about four or five fewer antlerless moose, or females, out of the twenty-nine that were usually allowed to be taken by hunters in those parts.

Bishop raised a hand and said the projected ratio of wolves to prey in the area was expected to be on the order of one to 378, so high that experts doubted wolves would have much of a regulatory influence on prey populations.

"They would simply be *swamped out* by the number of animals," Bishop said.

Weaver said it struck him as strange that there was no outrage expressed about the 5,000 elk that died the winter after the Yellowstone fires in the summer of 1988, yet hunters and outfitters continued to fret about the 1,000 animals that may eventually be food for wolves each year. Very little change was expected for prey species with wolves around again, Weaver said, aside from re-learning some of their old habits and instinctive behavior. Big horn sheep may stay closer to escape terrain. Elk might seek the safety of grazing in bunches.

"If there's any difference at all, any change," Weaver said, "there might be a slight tendency for elk to stay a little closer to the highway with wolves back—and, therefore, give the visitor a little more of a viewing experience."

The wolf is a preeminent large carnivore, fixed high atop the food chain, Weaver said, so pack densities here would be determined largely by the amount and type of vulnerable prey in the immediate area. The highest density ever recorded was about one wolf for five square miles. Weaver said Yellowstone could easily approach those levels in some areas. With as many as 22,000 elk wintering in the northern range alone, it was likely that six to twelve packs would establish territories in the area, adding up to a total of between sixty and a hundred wolves in this part of the park. Since elk were expected to be the wolf's primary food source—representing as much as 90 percent of the prey base—Weaver predicted individual pack size would be higher in Yellowstone than elsewhere. He attributed it to the weight of the primary prey species. While a deer can weigh about 200 pounds, elk are closer to 600.

"It seems like four or five wolves is a pretty optimal hunting unit for pulling down deer. If you get much bigger than that, there's not enough food to go around. Everybody's crowded around the carcass.

"Here in Yellowstone, with the primary prey being elk, there's likely to be more pack cohesion, less splitting off."

Weaver said the abundance of elk in Yellowstone also had a lot to do with the decision to reintroduce wolves to the park from western Canada, where there are existing populations of elk, rather than Alaska, where there are not.

"We don't want them to waste their whole lives here looking for a caribou. In Canada, elk are already one of the wolf's *search images.*"

Weaver said that one afternoon during his field study in Jasper he followed his wolves thirty miles in ten hours and saw them encounter three herds of big horn sheep, some less than fifty yards away, yet they kept right on going. Ever since, he has been convinced that wolves maintain a mental map of their territory and the vulnerable prey within it, that once they decide on a destination they have a single-minded determination to get there.

"The point of all this is that I'm not persuaded that in all cases when wolves are traveling that they're actually *hunting.* I think sometimes they have their minds fixed on something else and then they get in the hunting mood."

Class that morning was disrupted from time to time by the appearance of a single coyote looking down on us from over the edge of the next plateau. It was no further than twenty yards from us when it showed its face. Weaver played along at one point and put words into its mouth—

"*I'm going to send them my letter on the DEIS. I'm going to have my input.*'"

Coyote populations, Weaver explained, were likely to decline if wolves returned to the park because wolves were well-known to track down and kill coyotes caught in established pack territories.

"So when we bring wolves back to Yellowstone, you're going to see a few coyotes killed. Coyotes may avoid, to some extent, the most intensively-used areas in wolf territories. But you're not going to see a major change."

The red fox, Weaver said however, was likely to fare better with wolves around. Wolves appear to view them as less competition. Weaver said he once saw a fox trot right through a pack's den area in Jasper. Since they're fast and travel well over snow, foxes regularly follow wolves to kill sites to scavenge on carcasses.

"So wolves and foxes go together like ham and eggs. Coyotes get a little pushed out to the side."

If the coyotes were pushed aside, Weaver said, foxes, now considered rare in Yellowstone due to direct competition with coyotes, would likely increase in numbers. The impact on grizzly bears, Weaver said, would probably wash out in the end. He expected no effect whatsoever.

"I advanced a hypothesis a few years ago that wolves may actually be a benefit to grizzly bears in Yellowstone because right now the only time of the year when bears have access to ungulates is, for the most part, in the spring."

That's when bears come out of their dens and scavenge on the carcasses of animals killed by winter and when, on occasion, bears have speed enough to chase down a few young calves.

"But with wolves in the picture, there's a possibility that because wolves are killing these ungulates week in and week out the whole year, that bears may have access to some carrion in late summer and fall that they don't presently have."

Meat, Weaver said, makes a big nutritional difference for animals that have enormous caloric requirements to put on weight for a long winter of hibernation.

Later, when Weaver asked for questions, I asked him to describe how wolves would go about setting up territories where none had existed recently. I asked him if biologists were expecting a good many boundary disputes in the early going—I believe I phrased it *slam-dancing*. Finally, I asked him to what extent biologists expected wolf-on-wolf caused mortality in those early years.

"That's a good question," Weaver said, and I felt relieved, until he added, "but *nobody* really knows the answer."

Weaver said the DEIS did predict overall mortality rates would probably run as high as 30 percent among reintroduced wolves.

"There's natural mortality and we're going to have that when you reintroduce wolves to Yellowstone, just as you would have it for any wolves that naturally recolonize. So that's why initial numbers are so critical for establishing wolves here in Yellowstone. A few animals, unless they have a lot of luck, aren't going to absorb that mortality and still have some left over. So we have to dump a good number of wolves in here for several years to overcome all that natural and any human-caused mortality that takes place.

"You gotta keep pumping them in."

If the preferred alternative in the DEIS came to be approved, Weaver said, fifteen wolves from three or four separate packs in western Canada would be captured, collared and brought to Yellowstone each winter for at least four years. In a separate, simultaneous reintroduction in central Idaho, wolves would be *hard released*, meaning they would be set free immediately. In Yellowstone, the wolves would be *soft released*, meaning they would be held in secluded, one-acre fenced enclosures for six to eight weeks to acclimate them to the area and lessen the chance that they would leave the park to head back toward Canada. There were several reasons biologists preferred a winter release, Weaver said. There would be fewer visitors and sight-seers around. Mountain passes leading out of the park would be more congested with ice and snow. The appeal of breeding season would be fast approaching. Then, perhaps most importantly, the northern range itself would be a virtual supermarket of vulnerable, available prey for wolves. Fifteen animals, Weaver said, though, seemed to be about the most anybody wanted to try to handle at a single time.

"It's quite a logistical task to get many more wolves than that," Weaver said. "The point is to bring them in for consecutive years. That's the real key to the success of the program."

Weaver used the occasion to voice his opinion on the *natural recolonization* option outlined in the DEIS as well as to address critics of the *experimental* designation who believed recent sightings of wolves in the area had proved Yellowstone wasn't geographically-separate from existing wolf populations.

"A single animal does not constitute a population," Weaver said. "A population has to be a group of animals that interbreed, that have an age and sex structure, that have a genetic structure that persist over time. With this species, the fundamental unit of the population is the *pack.* Lone wolves do not constitute a population by any stretch of the imagination for wolves. Until there is more conclusive evidence that we have at least one, if not two, breeding pairs of wolves in Yellowstone, I and many other don't feel the area is disqualified."

Weaver said the recent sightings actually fueled biologists' hopes that there will be migration of wolves between recovery areas in Idaho and Montana, that some genetic interchange will occur through the occasional dispersal of animals.

"So, in one sense, the fact that animals are able to disperse down here from western Montana is good news. But the likelihood still remains extremely low that such dispersal could really establish a *population* here."

Bishop took a turn then to remind everyone that while there had been sightings of wolves in Yellowstone for decades, a breeding pack still didn't exist.

"Wolves have *popped* up, *popped* through, *popped* by," Bishop said. "But then they *pop* out, unless somebody *pops them.*"

On the walk back to the vans that morning, Weaver told me he was confident visitors would actually see and hear wolves running around Yellowstone once a population recovered. He personally guaranteed it. Because of the open terrain, he said, people in the Rockies stand a much better chance of seeing wolves than in the Great Lakes region. He stopped and pointed into the distance.

"Wolves are going to be traveling along Specimen Ridge here in front of us and I just bet you they'll come right down that ridge and they'll come down just along the edge of the timber and they'll pick up this road here and they'll either travel down that road or they'll travel there on the other side of the creek and they'll go on up Slough Creek."

A short while later, another student told Weaver he was concerned that too many gaping tourists would be attracted to the Lamar Valley once wolves returned, that it might cease to become the least-visited corner of the park, that the higher volume of visitors would affect the beauty, balance and character of the best part of the park. Weaver didn't appear the least bit concerned.

"I think the bigger problem is we have to keep the *geysers* out," Weaver said. "Don't let 'em transplant *geysers* up here."

The next field trip, to a small, shaded clearing beside all the babbling racket of Slough Creek, Weaver devoted entirely to the subjects of ranching and livestock depredation.

He began by citing statistics from the pages of our orange binders. The proposed recovery area itself, he said, for instance, included two national parks and six national forests, a 12,000 square mile core of wild country where no livestock was ever grazed during the year. While there were almost 400 grazing allotments defined within the recovery area—accommodating something like 145,700 cows and calves, 265,000 sheep and lambs and 1,300 horses, primarily during the four months between July and October—very few of those allotments bordered the park directly. Weaver then steered us to a map of the region indicating locations of the allotments. The closest were south and southwest of the park where, Weaver said, there were fewer wild ungulates present and fewer wolves likely to roam, and likewise, fewer livestock depredations likely to happen.

"The amazing thing is that wolves don't kill more livestock than they do, because they're obviously capable of doing so."

He said there was ample documentation of instances in Minnesota, Montana and Canada where wolves were living, more or less, in direct proximity to livestock entirely without incident.

"I'm not sure there *is* a pattern behind depredation. That's part of the problem. Why wolves prey on livestock some of the time, why certain wolves do it and others don't, I think for the most part is still unpredictable. That's why management has to be flexible. Wolves might prey on livestock one year and not do it the next year. It seems to be a very localized problem when it does happen."

Weaver said there is a chance wolf pups sometimes learn to include livestock among their search images as they are taught hunting skills and food preferences by their parents and pack mates.

"It's also possible that wolves may pick up the habit of preying on living livestock from having fed on livestock carcasses that haven't been properly disposed of."

Whatever the cause, Weaver said it was almost certain to happen around Yellowstone eventually.

"But it certainly will not have any measurable effect on the livestock industry."

Weaver then surveyed provisions included in the DEIS for coping with the problem. On both public and private lands, ranchers would be allowed to harass wolves away from their stock in a *non-injurious* manner—such as with honking horns or shooting over their heads—so long as they reported the incident to authorities within fourteen days. Wolves actually caught in the act of killing or wounding livestock on private land could be killed by ranchers, so long as they reported the incident within twenty-four hours and provided evidence of damage. Without such evidence, the rancher would be subject to fines, imprisonment and loss of permits to use public lands. In the event of the depredation of cattle grazing on public lands, ranchers could apply for a permit to kill wolves only after the governing agency with immediate jurisdiction there failed to solve the problem with prescribed control actions.

"I consider that a pretty remote possibility," Weaver said. "He doesn't get a *carte blanche* permit to kill any wolves that he sees on his allotment forevermore. He gets a permit to take those same wolves that the agency personnel were attempting to take anyway."

For the sake of argument, the class took a straw poll then and, to the surprise of many, nine students voted in favor of allowing ranchers to shoot wolves on private land. Five voted against. One or two of the supporters said they thought it was pointless to try to *micromanage* the actions of ranchers on their own land, that despite anything the law may spell out, they were likely to do what they wanted in the end anyway. At least with this arrangement, it would be above board, it might diminish resistance and, essentially, give them no excuse *not* to participate in the plan.

A similar vote concerning ranchers shooting wolves on public lands, however, was virtually unanimous against. Not one student expressed support for the idea, even in the event a wolf was caught in the act of attacking a cow. Time and again, students they said it was the rancher's choice to put his cattle there and, time and again, they said they thought grazing allotments should be curtailed in the area anyway.

Askins, who said her group was conducting an internal debate on the same issue in response to the release of the DEIS, said she found the results of the class vote revealing.

"Most of us know that you can't impose control on ranchers. The more you say—'*You can't take care of the problem. We'll take care of it for you*'—the more rage it engenders. And we know that rage kills wolves."

What she suggested, instead, was a practical approach to enforcement.

"Early on we have to have a management policy that's much more prohibitive and favors protection of the animal above the livestock. As wolves recover, you might begin to relax that protection so that ranchers have a little more latitude. I think, in general, people can understand that philosophy. They can understand that you have to be more guarded early on."

Some students, however, still worried openly about leaving ranchers too much of a loophole. Kaminski, the former Congressional aide, disagreed.

"You have to look at the incentive for them to participate. If the goal is to have wolves back and they don't disagree with that, you ought to allow them some flexibility on their own land."

Animals caught in the act of killing livestock, he said, may not be of long-term benefit to wolf recovery anyway.

"It may not be an animal that you necessarily want around and contributing habits, if you will, of that kind to its progeny. On private land, my view is that it's a worthwhile thing to do."

Weaver once took us on a long, morning hike up Specimen Ridge overlooking all of the Lamar to show us the big picture, which, in addition to scenery, meant politics, which happened to be Kaminski's and Askins's particular field of expertise.

Kaminski, who sat crouching low over his heels, staring down at his hands, said what always struck him as odd about the wolf controversy was that, as a policy matter, it had progressed only by default. He said the government agencies with direct responsibility to examine it as a wildlife management issue always had both the jurisdiction and authority to deal with it yet, due to political maneuvering, it entered a messy public arena and dragged on for twenty years. The DEIS process itself didn't get started, he said, until Congressional staffers prodded the agencies into doing their jobs and following a process clearly defined in federal law.

"I view it as a *sad* commentary," he said.

Askins, who was sitting in the sun with two of her staff members nesting behind her, said the most fascinating thing that had been revealed to her through the years was a modern phenomenon called an *issue public.*

"It's the idea that there are limited constituencies that may be very, very, *very* small but they have disproportionate power on public issues due to their political influence. That's really what's playing in Yellowstone wolf recovery in that there's a very, very small constituency that's opposed to it that has managed both to obstruct it and to set the agenda in which the debate takes place.

"I think that's really what has broken down in the last three or four years. That's where we've made a lot of progress," Askins said. "We've managed to take the issue back to the fifty yard line."

When it was Weaver's turn to speak again, he said conservationists, in recent years, had good reason to be more optimistic about the prospect of wolf recovery in Yellowstone.

"You folks are taking this course at a more encouraging time in the whole history of it," he said. "We're not quite as glum, as we were five years ago.

"What impresses me about all this is that I can think of no other reintroduction of any animal anywhere in the world that has had as much prior analysis of such a high caliber as what we're talking about for wolves here in Yellowstone. Every question that's been raised, Congress has commissioned a study to address it."

On another afternoon, Weaver led the group on a short walk from the Institute up a ridge to sit and talk near a spot that for years had been discussed as one of possible locations for a soft-release pen if wolves were ever to be returned to Yellowstone. I remember bright sun and a breeze, that it felt both hot and cold there at once.

We were to be joined in time by a high official presence, Wayne Brewster, leader of the wolf management team now deeply embroiled in the DEIS process. Before he arrived, perhaps to encourage us to be on our best behavior, Weaver told us Brewster used to run the Endangered Species office in Helena, that he then worked as a wolf management specialist in Glacier National Park before coming to Yellowstone. I also happened to know by then that Brewster was one in the handful of federal officials who crowded around Ray Paunovich's film-editing table a year earlier to get a first look at the creature Paunovich had photographed in the Hayden Valley, that it was Brewster himself who had returned to the scene with Paunovich the next day to locate and measure tracks. When he came up the hill behind the institute that afternoon, Brewster was dressed in street clothes, clean jeans, cowboy boots and a leather belt with his name, *W A Y N E*, tooled between his hips. He was pretending at first to be a lost tourist.

Weaver and he jawed and joshed for a few moments. They talked about all the long hair they used to have when they first started out. Once they got down to business, though, it was widely apparent that Brewster and Weaver were both old hands at this sort of thing. By the way Weaver always smiled askance at Brewster, I got a sense that he was only playing the objective devil's advocate here, that he already knew most of Brewster's possible responses ahead of time, that he was acting the part of a country lawyer questioning a friendly witness for the benefit of a jury.

Weaver asked Brewster, for instance, about *zone concepts*, how they were incorporated into recovery plans for grizzly bears in Yellowstone as well as earlier drafts of the wolf proposal. Yet, Weaver said, he noticed they weren't included in the DEIS.

"There's no attempt to try to delineate zones and set off differential management," Brewster answered.

"Why not?"

"Let me answer your first question first," Brewster said. "Why don't you just identify a *no-cattle* zone? Well, when you look at the evidence, very few wolves prey on livestock and those that do represent a very small number. So it's pretty hard to build a case that you have to move all of the livestock off an area if you can have a program that will address the livestock owners' concerns as far as responding to depredations. What that does is it allows you a lot more territory that wolves can be in *with* livestock.

There's very strong public and political resistance to closing huge amounts of public land because of *one* species. That's just the way it is.

"I guess it's a point that could be argued indefinitely. But if you carry the idea that wolves can have a place and they don't necessarily exclude every other activity or value that people want, then there's no reason why you couldn't have wolves clear down the Wyoming Range.

"If you start with the tenet that everybody else has to go because wolves are coming, then you draw the battle line. You pretty much stick the lance in the sand then. Truth is, you really can't predict where wolves are going to go. You can take a stab at it. You can say that you're going to have a fairly dense wolf population in *this* region. You can look around. But out and beyond that, it gets pretty iffy where things are going to be.

"My belief is that as long as you have red meat on the hoof you can have wolves anywhere as long as it becomes socially unacceptable for people to kill wolves and talk about it in the cafe and the bars and brag about it. You have to get to the point where illegal killing of wolves is just like child abuse. If you do it, you can't tell anybody."

Weaver then barely mentioned mountain lions and Brewster was off and running again.

"That's a good example," Brewster said. "If you look at the what they eat and what the problems are, there really isn't that much difference between wolves and mountain lions. They live on big game animals, they occasionally kill livestock, they occasionally kill people—which wolves *don't*. Over the last twenty some years, lions have repopulated almost every timbered area in Montana. All of these isolated mountain ranges have mountain lions in them, and it's happened with very little public furor.

"Mountain lions often kill livestock—that never even shows up in the newspaper. But let a wolf kill a cow and it's on the front page above the fold. It's just what people are used to. I think as people get used to the idea of having wolves and as they find out that they aren't the prince of darkness, then they'll kind of slack off. It's just that people need to get used to the idea of having wolves around."

Weaver asked Brewster about the advantages and disadvantages of allowing ranchers to harass wolves.

"The *cons* are few on private land," Brewster said. "On private land, basically, it's free aversive conditioning to allow people to harass wolves off of areas where they don't want them. If they stayed around they'd probably end up illegally killing them."

Askins interrupted and asked—"So what about the argument that giving ranchers *any* latitude narrows that line between shooting above a wolf's head and shooting the wolf? Even more, if it increases the possibility of illegal killing on *public* land?"

"Well," Brewster replied, "if you're in a remote allotment and you have wolves in and around your stock, you're probably going to harass them anyway. This gives you a legal option rather than just checking very carefully to see if anyone's around and then just killing them outright. That's the rationale for it. The idea is to harass wolves away from livestock. If they're hanging in an area and there's no reason for them to be there, then you're reinforcing a behavior in the wolves to stay away from people and stay away from livestock. That's the rationale for it."

Weaver asked about the preference of some groups to see wolves reintroduced without the *experimental* provision, to see that Yellowstone's wolves received the full protection of the Endangered Species Act.

"What's your opinion of the political viability of *that* alternative?" Weaver asked.

"I don't think it has much chance at all," Brewster said. "Some people argue that the *experimental* provision is illegal or is somehow going against the Endangered Species Act. I think the contrary is true. Congress specifically wrote it in to address really controversial species and reintroductions. I think if you ignore that provision and don't use it to achieve the objective, then you're proving that the Endangered Species Act *doesn't* work—and that's the one thing that a lot of the opponents want to *prove.*"

Weaver asked Brewster if he thought legal challenges could still stop wolf recovery.

"That'll delay it, but I don't see any biological or procedural holes in the process. Otherwise, I wouldn't be out here chit-chatting. I'd be going off trying to fill them."

Near the end of the visit, a student asked Brewster about the ultimate goal of the recovery plan, if it was meant simply to restore wolves to a national park or if it was meant to be a catalyst for wolf recovery throughout the West. He wanted to know if the plan was meant to restore the landscape more fully for future generations of Americans with a population of wolves that might remain viable for, say, the next 500 years.

"Well, at five hundred and fifty years of age my eyesight will probably be pretty dim," Brewster replied. "I think if you try to project five hundred years out you're pretty arrogant. I think you can *wish* five hundred years out.

"I think restoring wolves to Yellowstone is saying a lot about land ethics. It's saying a lot about the conservation of animals that require something of *us* for them to be here. Beyond that, it's absolute pure speculation and it would be my values, which are no better, no worse than anyone else's. I think all you can hope for is to buy time for some new generation to take it to the next level."

Saturday night at the Institute began with movies in the old Buffalo Ranch bunkhouse. Actually, it was a brief screening of the footage Ray Paunovich had shot in the Hayden Valley almost a year earlier—and a simultaneous debate of whether we esteemed students, teachers and guest speakers thought Paunovich's critter looked and behaved like a wild wolf. Nothing close to consensus was reached that night, just more questions and curiosity raised than satisfied.

While I had the advantage of having seen the footage twice previously by then, I still didn't have an answer ready when Askins turned to me and asked straight out—

"Does *that* look like a wolf to *you*?"

I was sitting down, off to the side, leaning forward toward the TV screen with my chin in hand, my eyes glued and all I could manage while she was standing there, waiting, searching my face, was something of a foggy shrug. Hell, Renee, I didn't know, and, to this day, I still don't.

"I've *never* seen a wild animal that filled out, rounded and look, *look*," Askins said, touching the blinking screen with her fingers, "it's hard to see the face, and the hips and the tail are set real high. It's those *haunches* that bug me and the proportion of ears to the head. The tail is a little high set for me.

"Sure is *well-fed,* if he's a wolf.

"We don't know a gender do we? We've sort of decided it's a *he*," Askins said, laughing at herself.

Weaver grappled his arms around her shoulders from behind then, teasing her like an older sibling. Eventually, even through the silliness, he rendered his opinion.

"My first reaction when I saw the tape last year was how—like you were saying—how full the animal appears for a summer-time wolf," he said. "I *did* like the way this one moved, the action of its legs when it was trotting across the valley. It *moved* like a wolf. If I saw that animal in Jasper, I'd have no reason to say it *wasn't* a wolf."

"Even with that kind of *weight* on it, huh?" Askins said, elbowing him in the belly.

"Like I say," Weaver said, poking back, "that's one thing that does bother me, because *wolves* do slim down in summer."

Askins spun out of Weaver's grasp. She still didn't seem convinced. She said most of the wolves she had seen moved around too much to carry their weight that way.

"It doesn't look like it's been on the road a long time," she said. "Although, I would *love* to be proven wrong."

One of the other students piped up then to suggest it probably didn't matter much anyway, that the footage wouldn't have that much impact on the recovery plan in the long run.

Askins disagreed sharply.

"With the presence of this film and then with the shooting, the total perception in Yellowstone has been of absolute, monumental change," Askins said. "People's assumption became that wolves are already here, that it's a done deal. That was my feeling at first, too—'*So what?*' And then it hit. It became obvious *what.*"

In the darkness of about 9:15 that night, the whole group piled into vans and pulled out to go howling *en masse* near Soda Butte.

Howling really does serve a purpose, for both wolves and the humans who study them. Wolves do it, in part, to announce their territories to neighboring packs, in part, to find each other, in part, to bond socially and probably also, in part, just to amuse themselves. Until the advent of radio collars, humans had little better means above howling for finding and taking a rough guess at wolf numbers. Researchers have found through the years that wolves often respond better to the live voices of human howling than recordings of real wolves broadcast over portable tape players and speakers—although few people believe wolves are actually fooled by such feeble impersonations.

As we tramped through the sagebrush and dry grass that night, crunching, rustling and thrashing, Weaver said we might stumble across bison milling around in the dark, and, I'll confess, in that moment I was consumed with panic, imagining the sound and sense of thunder rising out of the shadows, of stars exploding inside my skull as I was stomped bloody and flat for tripping over an unseen creature's midnight snack.

"We're initiating you people into the wolf club," Weaver announced playfully. I looked around to make sure he wasn't taking steps to abandon us there. Instead, he switched into the booming voice of a *faux* game-show host to ask a question about himself in the third person.

"Trivia question for you—*When John Weaver did his wolf survey in Yellowstone back in the 1970s, how many wolf howls did he broadcast over two years?*"

It was too dark to see clearly if anyone raised a hand.

"*He did fourteen hundred*—With one response. One response."

He and Askins were elected to howl first to give the rest of us an idea of how it all was supposed to work, and Askins pretended to act shy. She giggled and said—

"This was *not* decided upon." Then she feigned in a squeak—"*My throat's a little sore.*"

So Weaver went it alone. Since we couldn't see very well, he said he was cupping his hands around his mouth to project his voice. Then it started, a low, slow gliss upward, that hung for a moment and slid down slightly like a descending, soaring bird. It was operatic and melodic, I decided. Pretty. After a pause, Weaver came back with a series of tones that melted differently into the night air. If there was a wolf out there to hear this, I remember thinking, it certainly should have found something worth answering in all of that.

Silence.

Weaver invited us all to join in then. He told us not to sing in unison, that wolf packs usually howl in bizarre chords, probably to heighten the illusion of larger, fiercer numbers to their neighbors. He told the young girls who were along to stand up front, to squeal high and fast like little pups.

Then, for the first time all summer, I howled, too. I had gone along on wolf howlings maybe a half-dozen times already, yet until then I always just listened and looked around. I don't know what it was that made this occasion, this place any different, but I surprised myself then and, again, many months later when I played the tape in New York, when I heard my own voice, just once, making a clumsy attempt to sound wild.

It seemed all the worse for what came next. Askins' voice overtook all others in a moment, rising higher, faster and louder probably than the rest of us there put together. Some tried to chase after her and failed and some, including me, dropped out as she kept going until she was working a solo. Eventually, only once the spirit seemed to nudge her so, Askins let herself slide down a variant scale.

We heard coyotes answering her. Distinctly coyotes. On the tape I heard a high tremolo and I remember someone standing right beside me turning to the ridge to point.

Askins seized the initiative and launched into an eloquent, quick, diverse spilling of tones and barks, like she was fluent in coyote-speak, like she was a computer modem that upon hearing the proper response launched into a sequence of pitches almost indecipherable to the naked ear. There was laughter and astonishment expressed as we all listened after her, as she fired a series of squeals and screams that hardly sounded human, stuff that seemed to start in her toes and shoot straight up out her throat with her head thrown back, like bottle rockets and sparklers, as if they were physical objects with shock waves rather than just sounds.

In the end, there was only silence again from the ridge. It was almost as if she shamed the critter and it had run off into the gloom, tail tucked.

"Convinced?" Weaver said through a laugh.

Then, in the opposite direction, off toward the road, we heard a single voice, obviously human, rising and howling back at us. There was laughter at the suggestion that Askins may have persuaded a passerby that she was the genuine article.

It turned out to be Kaminski, trying a prank. For a minute or so, while he and Askins dueled in the dark, it struck me as odd that I was standing here, listening to two humans masquerading as wolves in the dark, howling back and forth in the wilds where, for the moment, there were still no real wolves present—or willing, at least—to answer. In time, though, I heard Weaver shuffle over to

Askins and whisper into her ear. They both fell out laughing and she asked back—

"Should I?"

"*Yeah.*" Weaver was laughing so hard the word came out shaped funny.

Askins took a series of deep breaths and, without notice, shrieked like a jungle chimpanzee, complete with *who-whos* and *ha-has* and *hees*, so loud it peaked off my tape meter when I listened again in New York. She couldn't keep it up very long, though. I heard her double-over from giggling and I imagine she could have been pushed over with ease if Weaver had only thought of it.

"*Great.* Ya'll passed the course"—Weaver said once we got back to the vans without incident. Kaminski was long gone, though, long before we got there. Someone suggested it was because he wanted to be able to say afterwards that he was never there, that it really was a wolf.

"Nah," Askins said. "He's just embarrassed because I *whupped* his ass."

The next morning, Sunday, Weaver told me about the last day of his doctoral study up in Jasper—and I remember thinking all the while of Ron Schultz way back in Wisconsin.

"When I finished up my field work up there and was leaving the park for the final time driving south, I saw a wolf right along the highway and we howled back and forth to each other for, oh, twenty minutes.

"It was a single wolf and it was off across this meadow about a quarter of a mile away.

"I saw it over there so I stopped and got out of my car and howled to it. And it howled back. And I howled back.

"I was the only one on the highway. And we howled back and forth to each other for like, thirty times, and I was the one who finally had to break it off because I had to get home.

"It was sitting on its haunches. Every time I'd howl he'd howl right back," Weaver said.

"Who knows what that wolf was thinking."

Epilogue

Historically, rhetorical analogies between nature and society have too often been used to legitimate inequality and domination. The function of cosmopolitical arguments is to show members of the lower orders that their dreams of democracy are against nature; or conversely to reassure the upper class that they are superior citizens by nature. Whatever else our inquiry has achieved, it surely was not intended to replace one system of oppressive rhetoric modeled on physics by an equally oppressive one modeled on ecology. ... Once we begin to think in ecological terms, we shall soon learn that every niche or habitat is one of its own kind, and that its demands call for a careful eye to its particular, local, and timely circumstances. The Newtonian view encouraged hierarchy and rigidity, standardization and uniformity; an ecological perspective emphasizes, rather, differentiation and diversity, equity and adaptability.

—Stephen Toulmin, *Cosmopolis: The Hidden Agenda of Modernity*, 1990

New York City

TWO QUESTIONS SEEM TO HAVE FASTENED ONTO ME IN SOCIAL situations since the summer of 1993—one while I was still traveling out West, the other after I returned.

The first was apparently a local custom, an inquiry commonly raised in place of saying goodbye in such big country, where distances make the easterner's toss-away phrase, *See you later*, seem absurd, in the least.

So, where you headed next?

More often than not, it was a trying question to answer with certainty. For something like 10,000 miles that summer, I lived out of the front end of a banged-up pick-up truck I had borrowed from my father back home in Ohio. Across seven states, my thighs stuck to black vinyl. I drove. I read. I took notes, napped and waited out rain. I watched everything and nothing in particular. Most nights, I slept outdoors in a tent with a screen ceiling arched to the stars. Most meals I cooked at roadside picnic tables and campsites on a one-burner stove. In back, my belongings—three spare tires, a five-gallon bucket of tools, three cartons of books, an old frame backpack and two pairs of dusty boots—were secured under a leaky fiberglass cap with bungee cords knotted about the tailgate. Dim, diesel glow

plugs often made for hard starts on frosty summer mornings in the mountains and, again, oftentimes, especially as
the thing shuddered and strained to face high winds and
steep inclines, great clouds of blue exhaust trailed after the
rear bumper like the tail of a poky comet. Passing on two-
lane roads on any terrain was always out of the question.
Even at rest, the parking brake had a habit of pulling clean
out of the dashboard—handle, shaft, cable, pins, all—so I
had to maintain a ready stockpile of rocks and small boul-
ders inside to lob under the wheels in the event that it
started rolling. Still, everything that mattered or, to cite my
father's standard, everything that was supposed to make
this thing move, seemed to be in working order.

Soon enough, and without much conscious fore-
thought as such, I came to nest in this space as if it were
my very own gypsy wagon. Up front, I decorated the glove
compartment door with a couple of refrigerator magnets I
found at souvenir stands—cartoon renderings of Smokey
Bear and Ranger Smith, Yogi's nemesis. I collected pennies
in a shallow compartment between the seats. I used the
rear-view mirror as a hook to hang my flashlights and a
fold-up candle lantern, the latter of which once melted a
stretch of plastic molding above it when I stayed up late
reading one night through a Minnesota thunderstorm.

Somewhere in Montana the following month I made a
discovery while driving that soda pop will bubble continuously out the thin spigot of a hiking bottle screwed down
tight. I remember imagining it to be spray tapped from a
geothermal spring, tasting soft and fuzzy, especially after
five hard days of tramping through woods and water.

Weeks later, in Wyoming, I squinted behind sun-
glasses into an afternoon glare shaped by crescent scrapes
etched into the windshield from bad wipers and shared the
highway ahead with a Native American man with a long
braid of black hair on the back of a Honda *Gold Wing.*
Swinging on a string from the dashboard in the breeze
from the open window was a white cardboard *CAMPSITE
OCCUPIED* sign I had acquired for a quarter the week

before at the Gros Ventre campground outside Jackson. All the way east and then south from Cody that afternoon I followed this biker and listened to a Count Basie retrospective on public radio. Each time the signal weakened and blended over to the next translator tower somewhere across the high desert plains, I cranked the radio dial slightly to fine-tune the new frequency. Time and again that day I lost and found Basie, just as I lost and gained ground on the rider ahead. It was as if he were towing the truck with a twisted rubber band.

I never wanted to go home.

While my tent seemed to change pitch according to the landscape each night, my father's battered red truck was a constant for me that summer, and traveling with it made me feel every bit as familiar, anonymous and insignificant in my surroundings as I ever wanted, and needed, to be.

The second question latched onto me in September, as I returned to New York, coming first from friends who already knew something of what I had been up to that summer, then, as word got around, from near strangers who were, in one way or another, all curious to know what it's really like to gaze upon wolves in the wild.

How close do they let you get? Can they really vanish into thin air? Does fear for life and limb ever cross your mind? Or are they really as gentle and friendly as people say? Does the sound of their howling at night really make your hair stand on end? What about the eyes, those piercing yellow eyes? Do they really cut right through you? Do you really get a sense that there's a whole, ancient soul reaching out to you from the other side?

I will confess that, as any storyteller is lured to a spotlight, I may have milked some of those situations—sometimes just a bit, sometimes for all they were worth—before I backtracked, before I always admitted, out of respect for both wild wolves and humans who spend lifetimes sometimes seeking them out, that I never did, and perhaps never will, personally lay eyes on the genuine animal. It is a truly rare thing now to meet wolves as they once were and, in rare places, remain. I've never been of a mind to hold that making the acquaintance of hybrids and captive wolves, pups and lone adults constrained by leashes, pens and questionable genes, ought to qualify.

Occasionally, I might try to argue that I also had logic, of sorts, on my side. I couldn't very well expect to see wild wolves in a place where they had yet to return *officially*, so, depending on how things looked for wolf recovery in Yellowstone from a distance at that very moment, I might hazard a guess finally that I must have been either very late or very early to see a real wolf out West in my time.

Eventually, in my reading, I came to feel something of an affinity with James Fenton as he entered into writing of a much different time and place in "The Fall of Saigon." (Be assured, I don't mean here to equate my experience in Yellowstone that summer to the Vietnam War, by any measure, just to affirm that reporters, first and foremost, are appalling voyeurs.)

> Although I had a few journalistic commissions, I was not going primarily as a journalist. I wanted to see a war and the fall of a city because—because I wanted to see what such things were like. I had once seen a man dying of natural causes, and my first reaction, as I realized what was taking place, was that I was glad to be *there*. This is what happens, I thought, so watch it carefully, don't miss a detail. ... The point is simply in being there and seeing it. The experience has no essential value beyond itself.

And later—

> Those who actually set out to see the fall of a city (as opposed to those to whom this calamity merely happens), or those who chose to go to a front line, are obviously asking themselves to what extent they are cowards. But the tests they set themselves—there is a dead body, can you bear to look at it?—are nothing in comparison with the tests that are sprung on them. It is not the obvious tests that matter

(do you go to pieces in a mortar attack?) but the unexpected ones (here is a man on the run, seeking your help—can you face him honestly?).

In the end, I've decided that if ever I should be so lucky as to have a brush with a wild wolf, I won't expect myself to write of it. I imagine I will adopt my own sufferable version of the local edict—*shoot, shovel and shut up*—that I will watch, be watched, and cache the moment away, gladly allowing it to remain secret, kept between me and the creature.

Selected Readings

Barker, R. 1993. *Saving all the parts: reconciling economics and the Endangered Species Act.* Island Press, Washington, DC.

Bartlett, R. 1989. *Yellowstone, a wilderness besieged.* Univ. of Arizona Press, Tucson, AZ.

Bass, R. 1992. *The Ninemile wolves.* Clark City Press, Livingston, MT.

Brandenburg, J. 1988. *White wolf: living with an arctic legend.* NorthWord Press, Minocqua, MN.

Brown, D. 1988. *The wolf in the Southwest: the making of an endangered species.* Univ. of Arizona Press, Tucson, AZ.

Chase, A. 1986. *Playing God in Yellowstone: the destruction of America's first park.* Harcourt Brace Jovanovich, Publishers, Orlando, FL.

DeBelieu, J. 1993. *Meant to be wild: the struggle to save endangered species through captive breeding.* Fulcrum Publishing, Golden, CO.

Dennett, D. 1991. *Consciousness explained.* Little, Brown and Co., New York.

Despain, D. 1990. *Yellowstone vegetation: consequences of environment and history in a natural setting.* Roberts Reinhart Publishers, Boulder, CO.

Fenton, J. 1993. *"The fall of Saigon": The best of Granta reportage.* Granta Books, London, in association with Viking Penguin, New York.

Fischer, H. 1995. *Wolf wars: the remarkable inside story of the restoration of wolves to Yellowstone.* Falcon Press Publishing Co., Helena, MT.

Fox, M. 1992. *The soul of the wolf: a meditation on wolves and man.* Lyons & Burford Publishers, New York.

Freeman, R. 1989. *Wolf hunter: ten years with a United States Biological Survey wolf hunter.* Common Man Institute, Gillette, WY.

Fritts, S. 1982. *Wolf depredation on livestock in Minnesota.* Resource publication 145. U.S.D.A. Fish and Wildlife Service, Washington, D.C.

Glick, D., M. Carr and B. Harting. 1991. *An environmental profile of the Greater Yellowstone ecosystem.* Greater Yellowstone Coalition, Bozeman, MT.

Gould, S. 1979. *Ever since Darwin.* W. W. Norton & Co., New York.

Halfpenny, J. and R. Ozanne. 1989. *Winter: an ecological handbook.* Johnson Books, Boulder, CO.

Halfpenny, J. 1986. *A field guide to mammal tracking in North America.* Johnson Books, Boulder, CO.

Harding, A. 1978. *Wolf and coyote trapping.* A.R. Harding Publishing Co., Columbus, OH.

Harting, A., D. Glick, C. Rawlins and B. Ekey. 1994. *Sustaining Greater Yellowstone, a blueprint for the future.* Greater Yellowstone Coalition, Bozeman, MT.

Hawbaker, S. 1974. *Trapping North American furbearers.* S. Stanley Hawbaker & Sons, Fort Loudon, PA.

Hawken, P. 1993. *The ecology of commerce: a declaration of sustainability.* HarperCollins Publishers, New York.

Hoagland, E. 1988. *Heart's desire: the best of Edward Hoagland: essays from twenty years.* Simon & Schuster, New York.

Keiter, R. and M. Boyce. 1991. *The Greater Yellowstone ecosystem: redefining America's wilderness heritage.* Yale Univ. Press, New Haven, CT.

Leopold, A. 1949. *A Sand County almanac.* Oxford Univ. Press, New York.

Lopez, B.H. 1978. *Of wolves and men.* Charles Scribner's Sons, New York.

Mann, C. and M. Plummer. 1995. *Noah's choice: the future of endangered species.* Alfred A. Knopf, New York.

Marschall, M. 1978. *Yellowstone trails: a hiking guide.* Yellowstone Association, Yellowstone National Park, WY.

Matthews, A. 1992. *Where the buffalo roam: the storm over the revolutionary plan to restore America's Great Plains.* Grove Press, New York.

Matthiessen, P. 1959. *Wildlife in America.* Viking Press, New York.

McIntyre, R. 1993. *A society of wolves: national parks and the battle over the wolf.* Voyageur Press, Stillwater, MN.

McNamee, T. 1984. *The grizzly bear.* Alfred A. Knopf, New York.

———. 1987. *Nature first: keeping our wild places wild and wild creatures wild.* Roberts Rinehart Publishers, Boulder, CO.

Mech, L. 1970. *The wolf: the ecology and behavior of an endangered species.* Natural History Press, New York.

———. 1988. *The arctic wolf: living with the pack.* Voyageur Press, Stillwater, MN.

———. 1991. *The way of the wolf.* Voyageur Press, Stillwater, MN.

Murie, A. 1944. *The wolves of Mount McKinley.* U.S. National Park Service, fauna series no. 5.

Pollan, M. 1991. *Second nature: a gardener's education.* Atlantic Monthly Press, New York.

Raup, D. 1991. *Extinction: bad genes or bad luck?* W.W. Norton & Co., New York.

Reisner, M. 1991. *Game wars: the adventures of an undercover wildlife agent.* Penguin Books, New York.

Rifkin, J. 1992. *Beyond beef: the rise and fall of cattle culture.* Penguin Books, New York.

Robbins, J. 1993. *Last refuge: the environmental showdown in Yellowstone and the American West.* William Morrow and Co., New York.

Russell, S. 1993. *Kill the cowboy: a battle of mythology in the new West.* Addison-Wesley Publishing Co., New York.

Sholly, D. 1991. *Guardians of Yellowstone: an intimate look at the challenges of protecting America's foremost wilderness park.* William Morrow and Co., New York.

Steinhart, P. 1995. *The company of wolves.* Alfred A. Knopf, New York.

Thiel, R. 1993. *The timber wolf in Wisconsin: the death and life of a majestic predator.* Univ. of Wisconsin Press, Madison, WI.

Toulmin, S. 1992. *Cosmopolis: the hidden agenda of modernity.* Univ. of Chicago Press edition, Chicago.

U.S. Fish and Wildlife Service. 1987. *Northern Rocky Mountain wolf recovery plan.* U.S. Fish and Wildlife Service, Denver, CO.

———. 1992. *Recovery plan for the eastern timber wolf.* U.S. Fish and Wildlife Service. Twin Cities, MN.

———. 1993. *Draft environmental impact statement: the reintroduction of gray wolves to Yellowstone National Park and central Idaho.* U.S. Fish and Wildlife Service, Helena, MT.

Varley, J., and W. Brewster. 1990-1992. *Wolves for Yellowstone? A report to the United States Congress, vol. I-IV.,* National Park Service, Yellowstone National Park, WY.

Weaver, J. 1978. *The wolves of Yellowstone: the missing link.* National Park Service, Natural Resources Report no. 14.

Whittlesey, L. 1988. *Yellowstone place names.* Montana Historical Society Press, Helena, MT.

Zakin, S. 1993. *Coyotes and town dogs: Earth First! and the environmental movement.* Viking Penguin, New York.

Acknowledgments

In addition to all those persons whose names appear in the text, I wish to express my appreciation

—first and foremost, to my writing workshop instructors: at Columbia University; Le Anne Schreiber, Richard Locke and Patricia Bosworth: and elsewhere; Leila Philip and Gretel Ehrlich

—to my visual arts instructors and mentors in New York: William Norton, Kana Oto Fuji, Aga Ousseinov, St. Clair Cemin and Judy Pfaff, who through steel, plaster and paint taught me more about establishing a dialogue with a work in progress than any other media I've tried

—to all of those who read, offered suggestions and rendered opinions on earlier drafts; beginning with my thesis readers at Columbia, Luc Sante and Michael Scammell

—to Michael Spooner and his staff at the Utah State University Press, who persevered, prevailed and, after almost a year and two complete revisions, tweaked yet a few more, important last-minute improvements out of me

—at the Yellowstone Institute: to the staff; Don Nelson, Susan Willsie, Michael Bartley and Pam Gontz: and to my teachers there; James Halfpenny, Don Despain, Scott Wood and Shane Thompson, the latter two of whom saw me safely out of the Lamar backcountry after I trashed my knee that August

—to all those associated with wolf research at Vermilion Community College and the International Wolf Center in Ely, Minnesota: particularly Dan Groebner, Lori Schmidt, Dan Armstrong, Trina Oakley, Wendy Vandepol, Tim Nichols and Bob Rintala

—to Hank Harrington and everyone associated with the Environmental Writing Institute hosted by the Teller Wildlife Refuge and sponsored by the writing program at the University of Montana

—to all who gave me either their time or encouragement during my travels, over the phone or in person: particularly Ed Bangs, Molly Clayton, Peyton Curlee, Hank Fischer, Joe Gutkoski, Dave Hayes, Robert Hoyle, Molly Matteson, Sandy McIntyre, Thomas McNamee, Matt Reid, Lang Smith, Pat Tucker, Bruce Weide and Jill Welter

—to my employers and friends at the Film Division of Columbia University's School of the Arts, who provided me with companionship and grocery money in New York for three years

—and finally, to my dear friends and patient classmates in Columbia's nonfiction writing program, as well as a couple of littermates adopted from poetry and fiction:

Julie Bertles, Melissa Clark, Melinda Corey, Emily Dyer, Alexandria Faiz, Alison Gardy, Jerome Joseph Gentes, Lynn Goodwin, James Jay Gould, Read Gildner-Blinn, Jill Hendrickson, Jodi Lynn Honeycutt, Laura Kriska, Andrew King, Patricia Grace Limlingan, Edward Nawotka III, Catherine Park, Christopher Patton, Kim Rich, Lisa Sack, Risa Schneider, Michael Silva, Jonathon Simon, Helene Stapinski, Vendela Vida and Aleece Yim.

About the Author

Jay Robert Elhard was graduated from Capital University in 1984 and worked as a community newspaper reporter and editor in central Ohio for eight years before moving to New York City in 1992.

This, his first book, was originally researched and written in connection with his studies toward an M.F.A. in nonfiction writing from Columbia University in 1995.

He lives and writes now and again in Ohio.